FLIGHT:
The Rise and Fall of Charles Lindbergh

A play by

Garth Wingfield

SAMUEL FRENCH, INC.

45 West 25th Street
NEW YORK 10010
LONDON

7623 Sunset Boulevard
HOLLYWOOD 90046
TORONTO

ISBN 0 573 63247 2 Printed in U.S.A. #8217

BILLING AND CREDIT REQUIREMENTS

All producers of *FLIGHT must* give credit to the Author of the Play in all programs distributed in connection with performances of the Play, and in all instances in which the title of the Play appears for the purposes of advertising, publicizing or othewise exploiting the Play and /or a production. The name of the Author *must* appear on a separate line on which no other name appears, immediately following the title and *must* appear in size of type not less than fifty percent of the size of the title type.

FLIGHT had its world premiere produced by the Melting Pot Theatre Company (Larry Hirschhorn, Artistic Director; Sean Patrick Flahaven, Managing Director) at the Lucille Lortel Theatre in New York City on May 16, 2005. It was directed by Nick Corley; the set & projection design was by Michael Deegan & Sarah Conly; the lighting design was by Jeff Nellis; the costume design was by Daryl A. Stone; the sound design was by Jill B. C. DuBoff; the incidental music was by Lance Horne; video projections were by Brian Kim; the production manager was B.D. White; the production stage manager was Marci Glotzer; the assistant stage manager was Allison C.E. Mitchell; and the assistant director was Noël Carmichael. The cast was as follows:

CHARLES LINDBERGH............................Gregg Edelman
ANNE MORROW LINDBERGH......................Kerry O'Malley
REPORTER.......................................Brian d'Arcy James
ADAM KLEIN et al....................................Andrew Polk
FRANK BORMAN et al...............................Rex Young
BETTY GOW et al.....................................Victoria Mack

*****

FLIGHT was presented as a staged reading at
An Appalachian Summer Festival
(Gil Morgenstern, Artistic Director)
in July, 2003.

PLAYWRIGHT'S NOTE

This is a play rooted in history, though not strictly historical. Events and characters have been slightly rearranged, combined and, in some cases, imagined. In a few instances, characters have been placed at events they never actually attended. The alternative would be a documentary.

This we know for sure: Anne Morrow Lindbergh wanted an introspective existence; Charles Lindbergh never wanted to be famous.

*****

The playwright is indebted to many works and authors in the research of this piece, including, most notably: *Loss of Eden* (Joyce Milton), *The Hero* (Kenneth S. Davis), *Lindbergh* (A. Scott Berg), *Lindbergh: A Biography* (Leonard Mosley), *Anne Morrow Lindbergh: Her Life* (Susan Herzog), *We* (Charles A. Lindbergh), *No More Words* (Reeve Lindbergh), *Autobiography of Values* (Charles A. Lindbergh), *The Wartime Journals* (Charles A. Lindbergh), as well as several volumes of Anne Morrow Lindbergh's collected letters and diaries: *Hour of Gold, Hour of Lead*, *The Flower and the Nettle*, and *War Within and Without.*

*****

For Jack DePalma

CHARACTERS

Actor One (male/30s or 40s)	CHARLES LINDBERGH
Actor Two (female/30s or 40s)	ANNE MORROW LINDBERGH
Actor Three (male/30s)	REPORTER (ALL) PRESS REPRESENTATIVE
Actor Four (male/30s)	ADAM KLEIN VALET THIRD TELEGRAM SENDER PHOTOGRAPHER SECOND LETTER SENDER GRAVEYARD JOHN SECOND FAN DR. ALEXIS CARREL HAROLD ICKES PRISONER
Actor Five (male/30s)	FRANK BORMAN AGENT FIRST TELEGRAM SENDER POLICE DETECTIVE FIRST LETTER SENDER DR. JOHN CONDON FIRST FAN HERMANN GÖRING RADIO ANNOUNCER SPOKESMAN

Actor Six (female/20s)	YOUNG FAN SECOND TELEGRAM SENDER BETTY GOW THIRD LETTER SENDER LOCAL GIRL THIRD FAN TRANSLATOR TWA PRESS AGENT COLLEGE STUDENT

"After my death, the molecules
of my being will return to the earth
and the sky. They came from the stars.
I am of the stars."

— Charles Lindbergh,
Autobiography of Values, 1976

"[Aviation] is one of those priceless
possessions which permit the White race
to live at all in a pressing sea of
Yellow, Black and Brown."

— Charles Lindbergh,
Reader's Digest, 1939

ACT ONE

"It all began with the Vicks VapoRub"

(As the house lights fade to black, we hear a popular late-1960's-era tune.

Lights up on a small stairway leading to a door on which there's a sign announcing:

"ATTENTION! No persons with any contagious infections beyond this point!"

ADAM, a young public relations representative, stands to one side. The song now plays tinnily through a small transistor radio near him. He holds a clipboard.

A NURSE in a white lab coat hovers over CHARLES, who sits on the stairs, with ANNE not far away. There's a large paper bag at her feet. The LINDBERGHS are in their mid-sixties, though this should be accomplished theatrically, not through makeup.

We're on the NASA grounds, just outside the astronauts' living quarters.)

TITLE PROJECTION: **NASA, 1968.**
41 YEARS AFTER THE FLIGHT.

CHARLES. No!

ANNE. Charles!

CHARLES. No!

ANNE. Oh, Charles...

CHARLES. I said *no*, Anne, so please let's change the subject.

ANNE. She only wants to peer down your *throat*. It's a wonder the young man here hasn't called Cape Kennedy security on us.

CHARLES. This is absurd!

ADAM. This is for the astronauts' well-being, sir.

CHARLES. This is a waste of time.

ADAM. It has to do with germs and infections. You said you felt sniffly.

CHARLES. I was making small talk!

ANNE. Calm down…

CHARLES. We never should have come here, Anne. I told you I didn't want to do this, and now I wish we could just *go*.

ANNE. *(a little firm)* Charles. Please. Let the woman look down your throat.

CHARLES. This is... Oh, for God's sake... fine.

(The NURSE moves to him and examines his throat with a tongue depressor.)

ADAM. I don't mean to force you into anything against your will here, sir. It's just, we're in a quarantined area.

ANNE. *(little smile)* We've had our shots.

ADAM. *(plowing ahead)* So if either of you has a cold or even cold-like symptoms, I'm not allowed to let you in there; can't let you anywhere near the astronauts.

(The NURSE stops her work for a moment and glares at ADAM, nodding toward the radio.)

NURSE. You mind?

ADAM. No. Jeez, sorry.

(He turns off the radio. She peers into CHARLES' throat again. Gulls call faintly in the distance.)

ADAM. *(to ANNE, re: the radio)* It gets kind of humdrum out here.

ANNE. I would think this must be very exciting for you, the launch and all.

ADAM. Oh, that part's tremendous. We're still on track to have a man on the moon by this summer, y'know.

NURSE. *(to ADAM, her business done)* He's fine.

CHARLES. I'm glad you think so.

ADAM. It was just a precaution. Thanks for bearing with us.

(The NURSE goes.)

ANNE. *(calling after her)* Thank you...!

ADAM. *(scanning his clipboard)* So, okay... um, what's your name?

ANNE. Lindbergh. Mr. and Mrs. Charles Lindbergh.

ADAM. *(absently, as he scans)* Right, right. You folks must be pretty important. Only a handful of VIPs actually get to visit the astronauts' private living quarters.

ANNE. Is that so?

ADAM. Sure, only the major big-wigs get to come back here. *(off his list)* I'm sorry, what's that name again?

ANNE. Lindbergh.

CHARLES. So who else has been here?

ANNE. *(under her breath)* Charles.

CHARLES. I'm serious, if you don't mind, um — I'm sorry, we didn't get *your* name.

ADAM. Oh, it's Adam. Adam Klein.

CHARLES. Yes, if you don't mind, Mr. Klein... who've you met?

ADAM. That's top secret, sir.

CHARLES. C'mon, Mr. Klein, we won't spill the beans.

(Little beat)

ADAM. *(hushed, fast)* Okay. Let's see. Arte Johnson — from "Laugh In?" — he was here just yesterday. And I've met Lulu. And Evel Knievel. This is off the top of my head.

ANNE. Really.

ADAM. *(off his list again)* Oh. Oh, Lindbergh. Here you are.

(The door to the building opens and FRANK BORMAN enters. He wears a jumpsuit with a NASA insignia embroidered over the left breast. A TV REPORTER follows him.)

BORMAN. *(to the REPORTER)* And the three of us are praying with the NASA chaplain at six this evening, you'll definitely want to get that… *(noticing CHARLES, a bit stunned)* Well, hello there. *Hello!* Oh my God, sir, this is so… *(then, fast)* I'm Frank Borman.

CHARLES. Ah, yes...

BORMAN. Did you folks just arrive?

CHARLES. We did. This is my wife, Anne.

BORMAN. *(extending his hand)* Ma'am.

ANNE. Hello.

BORMAN. *(a little overcome still)* This is... well… *(to the REPORTER)* These are the Lindberghs. They've come all the way from Hawaii to have lunch with the other astronauts and me.

ANNE. We're simply delighted you asked us.

TV REPORTER. *(amazed)* Lindbergh...

CHARLES. *(offering his hand)* Yes, um, it's very nice to...

BORMAN. *(overlapping)* This gentleman is from NBC News in New York. He's doing a piece on our launch.

CHARLES. *(then, clearly rattled)* A reporter…

ANNE. Oh, we don't own a television. I'm so sorry we'll miss your story.

TV REPORTER. This is, um... you're Charles Lindbergh.

CHARLES. *(hesitates, then)* I… I am…

TV REPORTER. My God. Now *you* were a great story!

(Pause)

CHARLES. C'mon, I'd hardly...

TV REPORTER. *(overlapping, to BORMAN)* Not that *you* aren't! You're a very... workmanlike story. True, if your mission was actually going *to* the moon and not just circling around it, you'd be a *better* story. But… I should go find my crew.

BORMAN. You'll film us praying, then? With the chaplain?

And having lunch with the Lindberghs perhaps.

TV REPORTER. You got it. Mr. and Mrs. Lindbergh, this was… You folks should get a television set. You really don't know what you're missing.

(He goes. Little beat)

BORMAN. You folks hungry?

ANNE. We're ravenous! Some dear men in research gave us packet after packet of freeze-dried space food to sample. But I think we'd prefer something a little more… old-fashioned.

BORMAN. *(to CHARLES)* You realize this will be our last lunch on earth before heading off into the sky. It only seemed fitting to share it with you. We wouldn't be here if it weren't for you, sir.

CHARLES. Oh, now stop that nonsense...

BORMAN. I know how infrequently you leave the islands these days, and, well… Captain Lovell, Major Anders and I are honored you came.

CHARLES. My... I… I don't know what to say...

ANNE. *(saying the words he cannot)* Thank you.

(Little beat)

BORMAN. Adam, would you escort Mrs. Lindbergh into the dining room.

ADAM. Will do.

(ADAM grabs the paper bag and leads her into the building.)

ADAM. Right this way, Ma'am.

(They exit up the stairs. A beat)

CHARLES. He's a curious man, that Mr. Klein.

BORMAN. *Adam...*

CHARLES. He actually had a nurse drive all the way over from the infirmary to check me out. A little pushy, but then again he's —

BORMAN. *(cutting him off; not wanting to get into it)* Yes, he's Jewish.

(A little beat)

CHARLES. *(little smile)* I was going to say he's probably from New York. If I had to guess.

(ADAM re-enters.)

ADAM. They're all set up for the next shot, Colonel Borman. The other astronauts are waiting for you.

BORMAN. Of course.

(BORMAN exits up the stairs, through the door. CHARLES and ADAM remain.)

ADAM. *(to CHARLES)* You're someone important; I feel like a heel.

CHARLES. It's alright...

ADAM. I'm an idiot that way. If you happened before 1956, I have no idea who you are.

CHARLES. Don't worry...

ADAM. So what'd you do?

CHARLES. Oh… Not that much really.

(The TV REPORTER re-enters.)

TV REPORTER. Mr. Lindbergh, I'm gonna kick myself later if I don't do this. I happen to have my camera — a quick photo — would you mind?

(He hands the camera to ADAM and stands beside CHARLES.)

CHARLES. Cameras… I don't think so…
TV REPORTER. It would mean so much.
ADAM. Smile for us, Mr. Lindbergh.
CHARLES. One second here…!
TV REPORTER. Just one photo, Mr. Lindbergh...
CHARLES. Not now, please —!
ADAM. Say cheese!
CHARLES. I'M READY TO GO!

(There's the bright FLASH! as ADAM snaps the photo — and then POP! POP! POP! A huge EXPLOSION of flashbulbs from the camera and from all around the stage.
Blackout. We hear "five, four, three, two, one," and there's a low rumbling, then a deafening BLAST as the Saturn Five rocket of Apollo Eight leaves the launching pad.
Then, in a pool of light, the TV REPORTER, dons a straw boater, becoming a REPORTER from an earlier era.)

TITLE PROJECTION: **NEW YORK, 1927**

REPORTER. *(out)* I'll tell you what fame is. It's fantasy, it's nighty-night dreams. It's authority, a demeanor that says, "Hey, I matter! LOOK THE HELL AT ME!" Valentino has that. Poor Little Gloria Vanderbilt? Ditto.

Perfect example: this transatlantic air race they've got going now. For my money, the only one with presence is Commander Byrd. Christ, the man flew over the North Pole! He smells like a hero. C'mon, you really think some air-mail-pilot-punk from St. Louis even stands a chance?

(At once, blackout except for a blinding white shaft of light. In it, a much younger CHARLES appears. We hear the deafening rush of wind whooshing past. CHARLES is oddly peaceful. He floats. He is alone, focused on the horizon. After a few beats of this —

A sudden shift — The ROAR of a HUGE CROWD! The shaft of light fades fast, another EXPLOSION of flashbulbs. A photo of the mob scene at CHARLES' landing in Paris is projected at rear, filling the entire back wall.

BOOM! It all stops, and we're back on the REPORTER in a spot.)

REPORTER. So I make mistakes.

(We hear a recording of the actual 1927 press conference. Stills and film footage run over this. The REPORTER, ACTOR FIVE and ACTOR SIX wander onstage, watching this, rapt.)

CHARLES *(V.O.)* "When I landed at Le Bourget, I landed with the expectancy of being able to see Europe *[crowd laugh]* but found that it didn't make much difference if I wanted to stay over there or not *[crowd laugh]* and I was informed that while it wasn't an order to come back home, that there'd be a battleship waiting for me next week."

(We hear phones ringing, typewriters clacking. The REPORTER moves to one side, where he's joined by ACTORS FIVE and SIX, who assume new roles. All three begin to speak frantically.)

REPORTER. *(starts first)* It's me. So he made it! The air-male kid flew all the way here by his lonesome. Who coulda guessed it? Now I've just gotta go in for the kill. I can do this. Don't sweat it. I'm telling you, I'm the perfect guy for this sweet little gig…

FAN. *(starts third)* Have you seen him? The boy is simply dreamy! He has a dimple in his chin and he's lanky and he's goofy and I THINK I'M IN LOVE! I'm going to marry him! I will be his, I know it!

AGENT. *(starts second)* Yes. I'll get it. Right, the deal. What do you take me for? Listen to me, this kid's golden! And the studio's mad for him, right down the line. I have six scripts sitting on my desk at this very moment he'd be perfect for. How's his skin, though? *'Cause we've got big problems if this kid's got acne.*

(Silence for a beat.)

TITLE PROJECTION: **MR. LINDBERGH SLEEPS IN**

(The AGENT and FAN go. The REPORTER lingers at one side.

Lights up on CHARLES, asleep in a Louis XVI twin bed at the home of the American Ambassador to France. The room is blue and gold, if we see any suggestion of it.

A male VALET stands formally nearby. CHARLES rolls around in bed a bit, then opening one eye and spying the other fellow, sits bolt-upright.)

CHARLES. *Qui... Qui...* darn. *(deliberately) Quelle heure est-il?*

VALET. *(consulting his pocket watch)* Nearly one in the afternoon, sir.

CHARLES. You speak English!

REPORTER. *(out)* There's one thing about fame, though: You can't take it to the bank, open an account, and expect to walk away and not look back.

VALET. Welcome to Paris, Colonel Lindbergh.

CHARLES. Yes. *Merçi.*

REPORTER. *(out)* You gotta keep making *deposits*, baby; not withdrawals.

VALET. Would you like some breakfast, sir?

CHARLES. That would be lovely.

(The VALET goes.)

REPORTER. *(out)* Take Fatty Arbuckle. The guy made a BIG withdrawal at the St. Francis Hotel in San Francisco a coupla years back.

(The VALET returns with a coffee cup on a small tray. He offers CHARLES the coffee.)

CHARLES. *(to the VALET)* Y'know, if you don't mind my asking... *who are you*? Did I somehow sign for this fancy treatment last night in some kind of stupor?

VALET. I work for Ambassador Herrick. He asked me to watch after you.

REPORTER. *(out)* The thing about Fatty Arbuckle is, you can't rape and *kill* a young woman in a drunken rage — or so the papers told us — you can't do that and think the movie-going public will look the other way.

VALET. Frankly, the ambassador was concerned for your personal safety given the conditions around the city last night.

REPORTER. *(out)* You can't do unthinkable *things*.

CHARLES. *(hazy)* I vaguely recall being shown the Arc de Triomphe by some very sweet men who spoke no English at all. And my French is, well, *mal*. Very *mal*.

REPORTER. *(out)* See, fame isn't just something you possess, it's a title you embrace.

VALET. I'll have breakfast sent up. Also, there's a reporter waiting to see you. The ambassador cleared just one. From *The New York Times*.

CHARLES. The *Times*; right.

REPORTER. *(out)* Fame is like a keg of gunpowder set beside a bonfire. You gotta handle it tenderly. You gotta tiptoe.

VALET. You don't mind, then...

CHARLES. No! Send him in.

REPORTER. *(out)* Don't get me wrong, I'm glad this kid made it to Paris first. Still. *(then)* I hope he remembers Fatty Arbuckle. *(turning to CHARLES, fast; big smile)* Colonel Lindbergh, I'm from *The New York Times.*

(The VALET goes.)

CHARLES. Come in. I don't usually greet callers from my bed. This must look mighty lazy.

REPORTER. *(little smile)* Hardly.

CHARLES. Would you like something to drink? Coffee, maybe?

REPORTER. Sir, I've been assigned to write a detailed account of your flight.

CHARLES. Now have you?

REPORTER. This is a very big break for me. I'm very excited. It's the first in a series of articles the *Times* wants to run.

CHARLES. Well, then. Let's talk about the plane.

REPORTER. That's not exactly the angle I had in mind, sir —

CHARLES. *(overlapping)* I want you to emphasize to your readers that this crossing I have made was not some isolated stunt, but a marvel of modern engineering. We have a specially made Ryan aircraft to thank, designed by Ryan Aeronautical Company — they're out of San Diego — with a gas capacity of 400 gallons…

REPORTER. Colonel Lindbergh, this story isn't about equipment. It's about you.

CHARLES. No, no; that's precisely my point. If you were talking to René Fonck this afternoon — if he'd made it here first

— you might have been able to write that story. Not with me, I'm afraid.

REPORTER. With all due respect sir...

CHARLES. Do you know what Fonck had in his biplane?

REPORTER. I don't.

CHARLES. A sofa bed. Do you know how much fuel that little luxury ate up?

REPORTER. I can only imagine.

CHARLES. René Fonck had Long Island duckling on china in a specially heated warming drawer. I had a couple sandwiches in a paper bag.

REPORTER. *(writing this down)* Brilliant!

CHARLES. *(snatching the pad away from him)* No! That's not how I mean it! *(Little beat, then, off-handedly)* Look. Aside from all this... in the rest of my life? I invent things.

REPORTER. Is that so...

CHARLES. Yes. I'm an inventor.

REPORTER. I had no idea...

CHARLES. Not aeronautics, nothing like that. I have other interests. So you can understand why I feel it's the *science* that matters most here.

REPORTER. So you don't want to be seen as René Fonck or Dick Byrd. With their sofa beds and high style.

CHARLES. They're valiant men…

REPORTER. But they wanted something different, didn't they? They wanted something that had nothing to do with science.

CHARLES. Fine; yes. Maybe they wanted to be…

REPORTER. *(then) Heroes*. Isn't that right, Charles? Do you mind if I call you "Charles?"

CHARLES. I'm a man with ideas, with plans…

REPORTER. Tell me.

CHARLES. I want to create new possibilities — biological, anatomical even...

REPORTER. Okay... go on...

CHARLES. I've done so much research on my own, I've read volumes. And now I want to study human organs, figure out how to preserve them. I want to get some sort of research post.

REPORTER. You do...

CHARLES. By preserving organs, see, I could learn how to correct nature's mistakes.

REPORTER. *(genuinely taken with this; writes this down)* You don't say.

CHARLES. *(unsure, almost shy)* It may sound unthinkable, heretical even, but I believe I could devise something better.

(Little pause)

REPORTER. *(low, smooth)* I could help you do that.

CHARLES. Yes, but...

REPORTER. Let me tell your story the way it should be told.

CHARLES. I'd rather focus on the facts of my flight, the engineering...

REPORTER. You can do anything you want once the world gets to know you.

CHARLES. I'm not Al Jolson! You want to make me into some character.

REPORTER. I want to make you adored, idolized! Look. So far, the world only knows you as some image in a photograph, a tiny figure waving to the masses.

CHARLES. Yes...

REPORTER. I can introduce them to the *man*.

CHARLES. Oh, come now...

REPORTER. The *potential* here, Charles, it's staggering! You *do* know how the city — for God's sake, how the world — has responded to what you've done.

CHARLES. I have my suspicions.

REPORTER. All of Paris has a hangover!

CHARLES. There were teeming crowds...

REPORTER. It was a madhouse! All because of the flight. Let's start with the final hours.

CHARLES. I don't want to be remembered as some dime-store adventurer.

REPORTER. Tell me something extraordinary. You almost crashed maybe.

CHARLES. Never! I flew for more than thirty-three hours without ever nodding off. I guided a sophisticated piece of machinery.

REPORTER. I'm making this up: You fell asleep at one point and woke up to discover you'd miraculously kept the plane aloft by guiding the wheel with your knees.

CHARLES. *(stunned at this realization)* You want me to lie. To exaggerate.

REPORTER. Not at all. I want you to *use* your experience. Six men have died trying to do what you have *done*. Everyone wants to know how *you* survived.

CHARLES. But it's the plane that matters...

REPORTER. I can help you. *(leafs back through his notebook)* I can help you... "correct nature's mistakes," as you say...

CHARLES. Oh, for God's sake...

REPORTER. *(earnest)* I can do this for you, Charles. You

know I can.

(A beat.)

CHARLES. *(then, vaguely)* There was Ireland.

REPORTER. *(energized)* Yes; what?

CHARLES. I don't know. I was tired, I'd been flying for, what, twenty-six hours? I saw a man in a boat, a fisherman. I shouted down and asked him where I was.

REPORTER. And...?

CHARLES. He didn't respond. Probably didn't even hear me.

REPORTER. Go on.

CHARLES. That was all. A few hours later, I landed in Paris. I'd seen a man, though. After all that time. It was vital at the moment.

REPORTER. It was a dreamlike vision; an omen of success.

CHARLES. It was a fisherman in a boat. I was relieved.

REPORTER. And you swooped down from the heavens — finally, human contact! — Asked a simple fisherman for directions and he stared back at you, mouth agape, all but *daring* you to make it to Europe.

CHARLES. No, no, no.

REPORTER. "Which way is Ireland?" you bellowed. And moments later, without even receiving an answer, you found yourself over Ireland. Right on course! How much later; an hour? We'll fill in that business later. You had hope at last. A sign of human life. This is powerful, Charles. This is good.

CHARLES. But that's not the way it happened. You're blowing things way out of proportion...

REPORTER. Charles! For God's sake, you can trust me.

CHARLES. I never said, "Which way is Ireland?" That's so phony.

REPORTER. Do you know the incredible value of a *Times* piece?

CHARLES. I want to work on my inventions!

REPORTER. *(with resolve)* What'd you ask the fisherman, Charlie?

CHARLES. I didn't do this for the publicity —

REPORTER. What'd you ask him?

CHARLES. I did this for the challenge —

REPORTER. *Charles!* Your wildest dreams are at the very tip of my pencil! What did you call out to the fisherman in the boat?

(A beat)

CHARLES. *(low)* "Which way is Ireland...?"

REPORTER. How's that?

CHARLES. *(bellowing, with considerable bile)* "WHICH WAY IS IRELAND, SIR?!"

(Another beat)

REPORTER. Of course you did.

(Random flashbulbs explode all around the stage: POP! POP! POP!
CHARLES shields his eyes, wraps himself in the bed sheet and goes.
The REPORTER moves downstage, filing his story.)

REPORTER. *(out)* Dateline Paris. "They call me Lucky Lindy, but luck had nothing to do with it. I have arrived to this city this morning to crowds the size and scope of which I've never witnessed..."

(The sound of a massive CROWD cheering rises, quickly drowning out REPORTER's report. MADNESS! CHAOS! The REPORTER continues to speak, though we can't make out a word of it.

After a moment, CHARLES rushes back in, holding a copy of The Times. *The chaos stops suddenly.)*

CHARLES. No, no, no — this isn't what I said at all! You… you've twisted my words around entirely! For God's sake, you've written it in the *first person*! I never agreed to that! And you've made me sound like some hick, some CARICATURE! *(utterly stunned)* If *The New York Times* can't be trusted to get my story right… Who *can* I trust?

(CHARLES stares at the REPORTER, who matches his gaze. Then the REPORTER snatches the paper from CHARLES and goes.)

REPORTER. And so we begin.

(A tinny recording of a popular song begins to play. At the same time, three TELEGRAM SENDERS appear and begin to speak.)

RECORDED SINGER.
From coast to coast

We all can boast
And sing a toast
To one
Who's made a name
For being game

Lucky Lindy
Up in the sky
Fair or windy
He's flying high

Lucky Lindy
Show them the way
Tell he's the hero
Of the day

TELEGRAM SENDER. Dear Mr. Lindbergh. Stop. You are a pioneer of aviation. Stop. Though I myself am in retail, I would like to subsidize your salary in these affairs of the sky. Stop. I will offer you one-hundred-thousand dollars to work as an executive at any airline you may choose. Stop. I can appreciate this is quite a sum of money, but I have no doubt...

(Lights up on a SECOND TELEGRAM SENDER, as they fade on the first.)

SECOND TELEGRAM SENDER. *(overlapping from "I can appreciate...")* You have no acting experience. Stop. I realize this. Stop. No matter, you are handsome and fresh and I am prepared to offer you a film contract totaling *three-hundred-and-fifty thousand dollars*. Stop. You will co-star with Mary Pickford. We will make you a star of the first order; you'll be adored the world over...

(Lights up on a THIRD TELEGRAM SENDER, as they fade on the second.)

THIRD TELEGRAM SENDER. *(overlapping from "We will make you...") One million dollars*! Stop. That is what I will pay for your world tour. Stop. The itinerary is yours to select, though your renowned airplane must land in the major hubs: Berlin. Madrid. Tokyo.

(CHARLES appears.)

CHARLES. *(awkward)* Um... no.
ALL THREE TELEGRAM SENDERS. *Damn!*
CHARLES. *(almost apologetic, as they head off)* Thank you…

(They go. Flashbulbs explode again all around the stage. CHARLES blinks, grimaces. We hear voices shouting out, "Mr. Lindbergh! Mr. Lindbergh!")

TITLE PROJECTION: **MR. LINDBERGH SPEAKS TO THE PRESS**

CHARLES. *(to an unseen throng of journalists)* I must say I'm not sure what to make of all the attention I've gotten recently. It's all very... you know, I'd really prefer if you call me "Slim." This whole "Lucky Lindy" business is so stupid. I wasn't *that* lucky —

— what's that, excuse me?

This isn't about my *mother,* I wasn't even talking about her; I really don't see why you'd ask that. She's an innocent school teacher. Why must you fellows launch into personal areas when I'm talking about something substantive?

And along these lines, I'm becoming upset — no, disgusted; I'm becoming *disgusted* — at the way normal citizens act around me now. Not two weeks ago at a picnic, these very civilized ladies scrambled in the mud to fetch a corncob I'd eaten. Like pigs, they scrambled. The house where I grew up in Little Falls has been vandalized, shingles and molding ripped from its frame. When I send my underwear to the cleaners now, I don't get them back. That's perverse! That's — and *you* boys foster this by asking me about drivel, writing up stories about insignificant matters. Please, the stories you write these days...

REPORTER. "Lindbergh Killed!"

(Suddenly, the REPORTER is there again.)

CHARLES. How's that?

REPORTER. Front page of all the major rags, Slim. November 25, 1928. One year, six months — and one-hundred-and-twenty-six interviews after landing in Paris.

CHARLES. *(remembering, smiles)* I was dead. Beautiful.

REPORTER. You'd been in Mexico City. After refueling in Tampico, you took off for what was generally thought would be Brownsville. As in Texas.

CHARLES. I didn't specify.

REPORTER. The point exactly. And when you failed to land in Brownsville, the worst was assumed. Crashed in the mountains of Mexico.

CHARLES. For a few blessed hours, I was actually deceased.

REPORTER. *(suddenly furious)* Jesus! Women openly *wept* on Fifth Avenue, Charles! Congregations all over the Deep South held vigils for you! And after it was over, once the rumors had been proven false —

CHARLES. *(hesitant, recalls)* I spent the night at a ranch outside Tampico...

REPORTER. Yes, yes! The masses were soothed as quickly as possible. *(then)* Did you know this? They stopped a performance of "Showboat" on Broadway! They announced the good news right smack dab in the middle of "Ole Man River." The audience cheered for ten minutes!

CHARLES. It *is* a rousing number...

REPORTER. Oh, Charles! You can't play these games! You have a responsibility.

CHARLES. To whom?

REPORTER. To me. To *them!*

CHARLES. So, what, I'm not allowed to escape for a few hours?

REPORTER. Not if it's going to upset the natural order of things! Slim, you want privacy. Fine, go off; be alone. Then — and this is the essential part — whenever you're about to embark on something newsworthy, *tell us*. You can even talk your science crap, if you like. Just don't hide. *(then)* You want me on your side, Charles.

(A beat)

CHARLES. And if I want you to leave me alone entirely...?

REPORTER. That's impossible now.

CHARLES. Suppose I retire or something.

REPORTER. You're not even thirty!

CHARLES. But this isn't what I bargained for.

REPORTER. Too bad. Too late. See, I know everything. Like, about that girl you've got now...

CHARLES. I don't have a girl.

REPORTER. Sure you do.

CHARLES. I'm a single man!

REPORTER. Oh, I know all about your girl. Don't lie to me, Charles. Don't play games with me. You want me on your side.

ANNE. There you are! I've been looking everywhere for you.

(Suddenly, ANNE is there. She's in her early twenties.)

TITLE PROJECTION: **A TASTEFUL AFFAIR IN CUERNAVACA**

(CHARLES moves to a stone bench, where two champagne flutes are set. A party is heard faintly offstage.)

CHARLES. Really? Is that so?

ANNE. Oh, yes.

(CHARLES shoots the REPORTER a look: "You can go now." Hesitantly, he does.)

CHARLES. I ducked out for some fresh air.

ANNE. I can see.

CHARLES. *(handing her a flute)* I got you some champagne.

ANNE. Well. Thank you.

CHARLES. You don't have to drink it. You can just hold it; a stage prop. Are you having a nice time?

ANNE. I think you're the one who should be answering that; this is all in your honor.

CHARLES. In that case, I'm having a splendid time.

ANNE. Good.

CHARLES. Your parents can throw one heck of a party.

ANNE. Yes.

CHARLES. Very tasteful.

ANNE. *(fast)* You realize everyone thinks you're after my sister.

(Little beat)

CHARLES. Elisabeth?

ANNE. I overheard some guests talking.

CHARLES. *(cautious)* Is that an accusation?

ANNE. *(realizing how it must have sounded)* Oh, Charles. No! Just an observation. I think it's kind of funny, actually.

CHARLES. Why would people think that?

ANNE. Colonel Lindbergh. Don't toy with me.

CHARLES. No, really, I...

ANNE. Honestly.

CHARLES. I just don't understand...

ANNE. I'm not insecure, Charles. But I *am* eagle-eyed, and I can see what everyone else can.

CHARLES. Meaning what?

ANNE. Meaning, for one thing, that Elisabeth is more beautiful than I —

CHARLES. Untrue!

ANNE. — and more outgoing and more bubbly.

CHARLES. What makes you think I'd prefer *that*?

ANNE. *(little smile)* Ah, yes. Pretty, charming girls are so unbearable.

CHARLES. Anne... I'm taken with *you*. Besides, you're more like me; like *I*; like *me* — please, you're the writer, which is it? *(softens)* We're very much alike, ya know? *(He kisses her. A beat)* I've never really had a girl before. This is all a bit overwhelming.

ANNE. After all you've lived through, I find it hard to believe that *this* is overwhelming.

CHARLES. Oh, but it is. I'd like you to marry me, Anne.

(A beat)

ANNE. Oh. Well. So you...

CHARLES. ... want us to be married. I've spoken with your father; we have his blessing.

ANNE. Yes, but, Charles, I'm not sure that I'm ready, that *we're* ready for... You don't know what your future holds.

CHARLES. True. But neither do you...

ANNE. There's not quite as much riding on mine, now is there? All I'm saying is, our time together has been very exciting — the visits in New York, your dashing down to Cuernavaca on a whim like this — but is all this — your life, is it really conducive to marriage? At this point? We should think this through.

CHARLES. You know, one of your cousins told me the only way I'd be able to marry you would be to give up flying. Throw away the whole deal.

ANNE. And what did you say to that?

CHARLES. I said... I'd gladly ditch it.

ANNE. But you didn't mean that.

CHARLES. Sure I did. If that's the only way to secure Anne Morrow, then my aviator days are behind me.

ANNE. Charles, I don't want you to give up your career —

CHARLES. I'll do something else. I have other interests.

ANNE. The thing is, I'm not sure how I feel about... well, this public persona business. I've had a taste of it with Father and government life, and… I'm a shy person, Charles.

CHARLES. So am I. That's why I want us to live quietly. Out of the spotlight. I rarely talk to the press these days anyway; I don't want to foster any more of that frenzy. I've had my fill, thank you. *(then)* I love you.

ANNE. And I, you.

CHARLES. Our life together will be humble, simple.

ANNE. I'd like that.

CHARLES. Marry me, and you're guaranteed years and years of utter boredom! That's the plan.

ANNE. That's very tempting. But...

CHARLES. But *what*...?

ANNE. I don't know, Charles...

(A little beat)

CHARLES. *(softer, warmer)* Do you want to know what I love most about flying?

ANNE. What?

CHARLES. The silence. You're up there, all alone, floating, and the wind becomes this... beautiful hush. You can bank, you can dip or just glide. You have the freedom to go wherever you like, anywhere in the world, and... it's perfect.

ANNE. I can imagine...

CHARLES. I can give you a life just like that.

ANNE. But please, what about all this attention you've been receiving —?

CHARLES. Oh, that's all dying out now! I can give you a quiet life. A very quiet life. If you'll only let me.

(They kiss again, as a vintage photograph of the Lindberghs is projected at rear, in silhouette against CHARLES and ANNE. They go as the picture dissolves into a series of photos: Charles and Anne in their flying regalia, the Lindberghs abroad, Anne holding a small bundle, and finally a photo of the Lindbergh baby on his first birthday.
BETTY GOW, a nurse, appears.)

BETTY. I'm not bragging but baby Charley could say "Betty" before he could say "Mommy."

TITLE PROJECTION: ***CLOSING THE SHUTTERS IN THE NURSERY***

(The photo fades.)

BETTY. I'm not making this up. I was his nurse; he was dear. But I'm getting ahead of myself. It all began with the Vicks VapoRub.

(A POLICE DETECTIVE appears. He places a microphone in front of BETTY.)

POLICE DETECTIVE. Please speak clearly so the stenographer can get everything, ma'am.

(She speaks into the mic, hesitantly at first. The POLICE DETECTIVE gets two more mics, for ANNE and CHARLES, who'll appear next. We hear all of their voices amplified, much like a radio play.)

BETTY. Mrs. Lindbergh and I were getting him ready for bed, and I'd smeared a whole mess of it over his little chest; Charley had a bad chest cold, see. So I go to get another Dr. Denton's sleeping suit for him and the only one that's left is unused and I think, Why soil a brand-new sleeping suit with the medicine? (Vicks VapoRub leaves a bastard of a stain.)

POLICE DETECTIVE. Go on.

BETTY. I take a piece of flannel from an old petticoat, cut it in two, baste the halves together and lay them next to his skin before we slide him into the Dr. Denton's. Works like a charm. Then I safety-pin the blankets around him so he can't push 'em off during the night like most babies do...

(ANNE appears.)

ANNE. *(overlapping from "So he can't push 'em")* I woke up that morning realizing I'd caught the baby's cold. Charley's cold. So I decided to spend another night at Highfields. That's our home in Hopewell. In New Jersey.

POLICE DETECTIVE. Gotcha.

ANNE. Usually I wouldn't stay there during the week and never without Charles; we'd go back to my family's estate. It's called Next Day Hill, and it's much more, well... secure. Anyway. Charles was going to be in the city that night and I didn't want to be alone so I phoned the baby's nurse to come up and stay with us, and she agreed to cancel her plans and come be with us for the evening, it was a huge relief...

(CHARLES appears.)

CHARLES. *(overlapping from "And come be with us...")* I was supposed to speak at some NYU alumni fund-raiser at the Waldorf that evening.

POLICE DETECTIVE. You were?

CHARLES. The appearance had been announced in the papers that morning. Everyone knew I'd be there. Well, everyone except *me*. My secretary'd written the wrong date in my calendar. It had been changed twice; it wasn't her fault. I called Anne and told her I'd be back for dinner...

(We hear a phone ringing.)

BETTY. *(to her)* Mr. Lindbergh is coming home!

ANNE. *(to the DETECTIVE)* To Highfields. A much-less-secure property than Next Day Hill. Everyone knew that.

CHARLES. I wasn't supposed to be there. I was supposed to be with the NYU boys. Everyone knew that.

BETTY. I had tucked the baby in.

ANNE. I was with her in the nursery. I'd tied on the plastic guards that would prevent him from sucking his thumb.

CHARLES. I was looking forward to a quiet evening at

home.

BETTY. I gazed at Charley, pinned securely into his bed. So peaceful, the boy.

CHARLES. I was envisioning a warm meal with my wife.

ANNE. *(to BETTY)* Mr. Lindbergh's due home any moment.

BETTY. *(to her)* I'll make sure everything's prepared.

ANNE. *(to the DETECTIVE)* Betty left.

(Lights dim on BETTY and CHARLES.)

POLICE DETECTIVE. And you stayed in the nursery.

ANNE. Yes.

POLICE DETECTIVE. All alone.

ANNE. With Charley. I turned off the light and moved to the window, closed the shutters, and made sure the window was pushed all the way down. I didn't bolt it because we're on the second floor; we never bolt the windows. It occurred to me later… I've been wondering ever since… if maybe that was some kind of signal to those without. "The Lindberghs are home today, even though it's a Tuesday and they're usually at Next Day Hill." Was it my fault? Did I tip them off?

(Little beat)

POLICE DETECTIVE. So you stood at the window.

ANNE. Yes. And closed the shutters. Charles came home and we had dinner.

CHARLES. How wonderful is this?

(In a flash, we're there. CHARLES and ANNE stand opposite one

another, an imaginary dinner table between them. The POLICE DETECTIVE steps into the shadows.)

ANNE. It's nice to have you here. It's nice to be alone together.

CHARLES. Are you as hungry as I am?

(The lights shift. The POLICE DETECTIVE emerges from the shadows.)

ANNE. *(to the DETECTIVE)* And that's when we heard the noise, the crash. We heard it the minute we began to eat.

(We hear a loud crash. Wood splintering? China breaking? It's hard to tell.)

CHARLES. What was that?

ANNE. I can't imagine.

CHARLES. Should we go and see?

ANNE. Hold on…

(They listen.)

CHARLES. Nothing.

ANNE. It was probably just Betty in the kitchen. Putting away the dinner things.

CHARLES. Of course. You know what I'd like to do after I eat? Soak in a bath. Is that decadent? Soak in a bath, then read. That's my agenda.

(The POLICE DETECTIVE moves to them.)

ANNE. *(to the DETECTIVE)* So Charles went up to his bath, and I wrote in my diary.

CHARLES. Anne's a wonderful writer — you should know this. She's writing a book, a chronicle of our trip to the Orient —

ANNE. *(forceful, "let's stay on topic")* Charles!

CHARLES. Right. I toweled off and headed down to the study.

POLICE DETECTIVE. Yes...

ANNE. And all over the house, there was silence. Stillness. Happiness. *(then)* Betty finished up for the night.

(BETTY appears.)

BETTY. I was just about to head out when I decided to peek in on the baby one last time. I don't know why. I worry. When I opened the door, it was freezing in there. I'd left a space heater on, so there shouldn't have been a chill. *(then)* I go to the crib.

CHARLES. I delve into my reading.

ANNE. I think I might like a glass of warm lemonade. For my cold.

BETTY. I lean over to pick up Charley, and he's not there. The blankets are still pinned to the bed just as I'd left them. Another of Colonel Lindbergh's childish pranks, I assume.

ANNE. I ring down for the lemonade.

BETTY. I knock on Mrs. Lindbergh's door. *(to her)* Do you have the baby, ma'am?

ANNE. *(surprised at this question)* No...

BETTY. Does the Colonel then?

ANNE. Why, I don't know. He must have.

BETTY. *(to us)* I go down to the study. *(to him)* Colonel

Lindbergh, do you have the baby? Please don't fool me; he needs his sleep.

(A beat)

CHARLES. I race up the stairs three at a time. I get to the nursery.

ANNE. I'm already there. Tearing through the closets, crawling under the crib. *(to him)* Charles, please tell me this is another of your awful jokes!

CHARLES. No, I... *(to the DETECTIVE)* I notice the open window.

ANNE. Lord, no...

BETTY. *(to the DETECTIVE)* The chill.

CHARLES. I dash outside. There's no sign of a break-in. The phone lines haven't been cut. WHAT THE HELL IS GOING ON HERE? I, I'm at an utter loss...

ANNE. Back in the nursery. Betty and I see something positively sickening.

BETTY. Mud stains on the carpet. Faint, but they're there.

CHARLES. I come back into the room. And that's when we notice — who saw it first? Was it you, Anne? God, I can't even remember.

ANNE. The envelope.

BETTY. On the radiator. A plain, white envelope.

CHARLES. Yes.

ANNE. So. Now we all knew what this was about. We had proof. We understood that it was a... I can't say the word.

CHARLES. I phoned the police. You boys arrived.

POLICE DETECTIVE. Yes.

ANNE. We didn't open the envelope, didn't even *touch* it

until you got here.

POLICE DETECTIVE. My men, they've... dusted it for fingerprints. *(gently)* Nothing.

(A little beat)

CHARLES. *(to no one in particular)* So that's where we stand. That's where we...

Someone has taken our child. Yanked him by his *feet* from his crib so, so *deftly*... that his safety-pinned blanket wasn't even rumpled! Who does that to an infant? These things don't happen! What's going ON here? Did I ASK for this?! AND NOW MY SON HAS BEEN STOLEN —?! *(he collects himself)* But there's so much work to be done...

POLICE DETECTIVE. That's all for tonight. You folks should get some sleep.

CHARLES. *(scoffs)* Sleep...

BETTY. Let me help you, Mrs. Lindbergh.

(CHARLES, BETTY, and the POLICE DETECTIVE go.)

ANNE. That night I dreamt of baby Charley. *(She steps into a shaft of light.)* I dreamed he walked into my bedroom, a fully grown man. So handsome, dimpled chin just like his father. Very dashing, very refined. Except that he was wearing his Dr. Denton's sleeping suit. Which still fit. Isn't that curious? I called out, "Charley, did your captors treat you badly? Did you have a happy life?" And he said, "Yes, mum, I've turned out quite well."

Which didn't ring true, since he wasn't British and we had no foreseeable plans to ship him overseas to prep school. Still. He looked at me with a sigh and a world-weary grin — he was wearing the plastic guards that prevented thumb-sucking, did I mention that? — and said, "You've no idea how *I* see this whole deal. *You* see it as a tragedy; *I* see it as an adventure. I'm meeting new people, Mum! I'm going out the window into the vast unknown."

It was infant-logic. It was myopic. And yet... it made sense. Early-morning sense. With the potency of the scenarios that rattle around in your head in the waking hours when you've barely heard the alarm ring and your nighttime visions seem eerily life-like.

My child! I'd never even thought about it from Charley's perspective. Sickening as it may seem, could it be that he wasn't sorry to leave us after all?

Which brings me to a disturbing fact I'd completely forgotten until I awoke the following morning. You see, the night Charley was taken? That whole evening after we put him down? We never heard him cry.

REPORTER. *(out)* Seven o'clock the next morning. *(wicked smile)* We arrived.

(The REPORTER is there. ANNE goes.)

REPORTER. *(out)* The Lindbergh property? Completely mobbed. Reporters and photographers by the score. The *Times*, the *Evening Journal*, the *Record*. Jesus, several photographers even arrived in a phony ambulance with flashing lights. Get this: It's a moveable darkroom, but it has a siren and everyone thought it was the real McCoy. It got past the guards! Is that sick?

And Lindbergh's gone and done something way out of character. He's welcomed us into his home.

(CHARLES appears, as do the REPORTER and a PHOTOGRAPHER; ACTOR FIVE and ACTOR SIX appear as well, filling out this scene as other reporters. They all shout out questions at CHARLES. Once again, there is an EXPLOSION of flashbulb pops from around the stage — POP!, POP!, POP!)

REPORTER. *(shouting out from within the throng)* Colonel Lindbergh, do you have any clues?!

CHARLES. A few, yes. The police are following all leads.

PHOTOGRAPHER. Give us a weepy mug, okay? Show some feeling.

CHARLES. How's that...?

(The PHOTOGRAPHER snaps the shot — FLASH!)

PHOTOGRAPHER. Got it!

(He exits with ACTOR FIVE.)

REPORTER. Lindbergh! How much are the kidnappers asking?

CHARLES. *(still confused; what just happened?)* Fifty... fifty thousand dollars...

REPORTER. And will you pay that?

CHARLES. Of course. I'll do whatever it takes to ensure that my son is returned. I'll grant interviews, show you around the nursery, give you photos. We've got a whole commissary set up in the garage, complete with coffee and muffins. All for you boys. I want my son back. I'm trying to help you here.

LETTER SENDER. Dear Mr. Lindbergh.

(CHARLES and the REPORTER go, along with ACTOR SIX. A LETTER SENDER, late teens, is there.)

LETTER SENDER. I'm a student at Princeton Prep School. My family lives right near you. On the afternoon of the kidnapping, I was driving down Featherbed Lane. I passed a car driven by a clean-shaven man in city clothes; in the backseat I noticed a disassembled ladder. And it struck me as odd because you don't see this sort of thing every day...

(Lights up on a SECOND LETTER SENDER, a middle-aged man, as they fade on the first.)

SECOND LETTER SENDER. *(overlapping from "And it struck me")* Dear Mr. Lindbergh. I am told I'm blessed with a gift. I have visions. And I am relieved to tell you that your son is alive, sir. I have seen him. He's in a small house upstate. He's being well cared for by a woman and three men. If you send me two hundred dollars, I will gladly tell his whereabouts, since I want to help you get your son back quickly, sir…

(Lights up on a THIRD LETTER SENDER as they fade on the second. She is older, with a thick Southern accent.)

THIRD LETTER SENDER. *(overlapping from "since I want to help you...")* Dear Mr. Lindbergh. I'm just a simple lady from rural Georgia. My husband works hard in the mill here. We don't have nearly as much as you and your wife, but me and Pete do have four healthy children. Our youngest, a boy, is eighteen months old, just two months shy of your Charley. Please don't think I'm crazy, but I would gladly donate my son to you if yours isn't found.

That must sound heartless. And pitiful. I mean it, though. Me and Pete, we've discussed this. We've got four good ones, y'see, and you've got none — *(catches herself:)* God forbid. I love my youngest dearly, but I want you to have him, and I'm not gonna tell you his birth name 'cause I'm sure he could answer to "Charley" in no time. He's only eighteen months old now, y'see.

Our son's yours if you want him, sir. Course... If you don't take to him, we'll gladly take him back.

(Suddenly, the REPORTER is there.)

REPORTER. *(out)* They received twelve letters like that.

THIRD LETTER SENDER. *(to him)* I meant what I wrote.

(She goes.)

REPORTER. *(out)* America's mobilizing around their cause. Support's pouring in from everywhere. You can't imagine the attention.

(One by one, characters appear until the stage is dotted with ALL SIX ACTORS. They talk to the REPORTER.)

CHARLES. And I'm cooperating. I'm working with the FBI, the papers. I'm practically running a field office out of my living room. Working together, you see...

REPORTER. *(to him)* Working as one...

CHARLES. Yes, working as a *team*, we can solve this. I pray.

(ANNE is there.)

ANNE. Some very unusual men started appearing in our home. Men with ties to the underworld.

CHARLES. *(to her)* We've got to explore every avenue, dear.

ANNE. *(to the REPORTER)* Still. Men who were on a first-name basis with Al Capone were sitting on our sofa. Flicking cigar ash onto our china saucers.

CHARLES. We were getting fake ransom notes and countless tips. Ordinary citizens were getting involved.

(DR. JOHN CONDON, a self-important, somewhat eccentric older man, appears.)

CONDON. *(to the REPORTER)* I wrote a letter to the *Bronx Home News*. I offered to put up, to donate a thousand of my own dollars to add to the ransom payment. This whole incident had affected me quite deeply.

CHARLES. *(to the REPORTER)* I suppose it was reassuring to know people were on our side. But still…

CONDON. I'm a retired public-school principal. Name's Dr. John Condon. I thought maybe I could do my part. I thought maybe I could act as a go-between.

ANNE. *(to the REPORTER)* We appreciated the outpouring.

CONDON. To my surprise, I got a letter from the kidnappers in the mail.

REPORTER. Right, the FBI received bags and bags of those. All of 'em phonies.

CONDON. But this one was marked with a trigamba.

(A little beat)

REPORTER. *(out, as if he's calling in his story)* You still there? Hold the front page.

CONDON. Three interlocking circles.

REPORTER. *(to him)* The note in the nursery'd had this mark, a trigamba. We didn't report it. *(out)* The good doctor's hit pay dirt.

CONDON. All I said was, I'd be the go-between if they like.

CHARLES. It was all getting so complicated.

ANNE. *(to CHARLES)* He only wants to help us, Charles. *(then)* Dr. Condon came to our home.

CONDON. I spoke with the kidnappers by phone. Several times over the next few weeks. The man I spoke with had a very thick Scandinavian accent. I met with him in person. In a graveyard. To arrange the details of the exchange. He said his name was John. He said the baby was being well fed. But during our chat, John also said something that made me stop cold.

JOHN. *(to him)* Vass if the baby ees dead?

(GRAVEYARD JOHN is there.)

JOHN. Vass if the baby ees lost?

CONDON. The hairs on my neck stood up. They actually did. What could I say? Worst-case-scenarios were racing through my head. I told him we wanted proof that baby Charley was well. In the mail, we received the boy's Dr. Denton sleeping suit. Freshly laundered. Sent off several days after our meeting in the graveyard. I was worried. Was Charley already gone?

ANNE. *(a revelation)* My God, was he dropped from the ladder when they took him out the window? Was *that* the crash we heard?

CONDON. Did Graveyard John go back to the place where they'd stashed the body, take off the suit, wash it, then mail it to us? Why would they *launder* his Dr. Denton's?

ANNE. *(pondering this)* Oh. My. Oh, no....

CHARLES. *(off her crying, or imminent crying)* Anne. We can't.

CONDON. Weeks went by.

(A LOCAL GIRL appears.
The REPORTER moves center stage. Everyone talks to him, from various places on the stage.)

GIRL. Have you heard the latest ditty? It's a novelty number, but everyone's singing it.

CHARLES. *(enraged, to CONDON)* Why haven't we settled this?! We're in touch with the kidnappers; I have the money. I WANT MY SON BACK!!

CONDON. We set a date for the final meeting.

CHARLES. I gave him the money.

GIRL. It's so cute. I'll sing it for you.

ANNE. I was hopeful somehow. Call me naïve. Maybe baby Charley would come home.

CHARLES. We drove to the meeting place.

REPORTER. *(writes in his notebook)* St. Raymond's Cemetery in the Bronx. *(then)* These people liked to transact business in graveyards. Go figure.

CONDON. I was looking for some sign of Graveyard John.

CHARLES. I was waiting in the car.

ANNE. I was pacing like crazy at home.

CONDON. I was listening. Nothing. Had he stood us up? That's when I heard him shout out —

JOHN. Hey, docktor!

GIRL. *(singing)*

Who stole the Lindbergh baby?
Was it you? Was it you?

CONDON. I walked over to him.

CHARLES. *(to the REPORTER)* I actually heard Graveyard John's voice. With my own ears. From inside the car: "Hey, docktor!" I had heard the voice of the man who stole our son. This was no longer some figment I'd imagined, some fantasy I'd created from sparse lines in a few brief notes. This was a man...

GIRL. *(singing)*

Who stole the Lindbergh baby?
Was it you? Was it you?

CONDON. I gave him the money; actually, twenty thousand less than he'd asked for. Let's just say I can negotiate. He gave me a note, chicken-scratch directions to where the baby could be found.

CHARLES. We went to this place. We flew there right away.

CONDON. A boat in the Long Island Sound.

ANNE. Could this be? Was our Charley coming home?

CHARLES. Nothing. No boat even.

(A beat)

ANNE. *(to the REPORTER)* We tried to press on.

CHARLES. It had all been some cruel goose chase.

CONDON. The papers suddenly turned on me, branding me a conman, some crook who'd scammed the Lindberghs out of quite a sum of money. That was for starters. Then they started saying I was in cahoots with the kidnappers, actually getting a cut of the loot.

GIRL. *(singing)*

Who stole the Lindbergh baby?
Was it you? Was it you?

CHARLES. *(to CONDON, suddenly suspicious)* Why *did* you get involved, anyway?

CONDON. I WANTED TO HELP! I was being selfless, BENEVOLENT! *(then)* Jesus! You don't know me. How DARE you pass judgment on me!

ANNE. And then, well, we heard.

(A telephone rings.)

ANNE. They'd found our son.

CHARLES. *(pulls himself together, then)* The police told us a driver had spotted the body when he'd headed into the woods to urinate. Charley was lying in the mud. On his face. Not far from our house, as it turned out, in an advanced stage of decomposition. Vultures had already gnawed away at him. His liver and intestines had been devoured. It was all, hmm… *(a deep sigh, then)* It was over.

ANNE. My son, my Charley was...

CONDON. Dead. After all that.

REPORTER. Tossed aside like refuse in the wilds of New Jersey.

CHARLES. And all I knew of the murderer was his voice, was his —

JOHN. Hey, docktor!

CHARLES. Yes. So. That was that.

GIRL. *(singing)*

After he crossed the ocean wide,

Was that the way to show our pride?
Was it you? Was it you? Was it you?

(Silence)

CHARLES. And I couldn't help wondering... What if I'd never flown to Paris in the first place?

(Sudden blackout except for CHARLES, who appears in a shaft of light as during the Paris flight earlier. We hear the thunderous whoosh of the rushing wind. Very loud! CHARLES is at once free, peaceful, transported. He stands there, basking in this memory. Then, just as suddenly as this moment began —
SLAM! Back to normal light. CHARLES is there alone with the REPORTER.)

REPORTER. So go on.

CHARLES. *(to the REPORTER)* Charley was taken to a funeral home in Trenton. Anne and I wanted him cremated. By law, they had to perform an autopsy. Christ, I didn't want to know *how* Charley'd been killed — what did it matter now? But. They did the autopsy at the funeral home. Took apart his tiny body. We discovered later that the undertakers had been drinking during the business, which meant an inconclusive report. Which meant more. Which meant they stumbled out into the streets of Trenton, waded through a few speakeasies, and bumped into a photographer from the *Daily Mirror*, who convinced the undertaker to go back to the funeral home and take him along. And show him Charley's body. And let him take photographs.

(A beat)

CHARLES. No newspaper would publish this trash, but still — it existed. These men actually snapped photos of my son's corpse. The very thought of that... is considerably more sickmaking than the vultures who'd picked away at his liver. *(glares at the REPORTER)* The vultures... What maniac does this?

REPORTER. They arrested a man, name of Bruno Richard Hauptmann.

CHARLES. Yes, *yes*! I'm sure he's the one who did this. I'm certain he acted alone.

REPORTER. There are questions.

CHARLES. Hauptmann is the one who killed my son.

REPORTER. I'm not so sure.

CHARLES. The voice I heard: "Hey, Docktor!" That was Hauptmann's voice.

REPORTER. There's evidence — a visible skull fracture, the fact that the body was so badly decomposed — that the baby really *was* dropped when he was taken down the ladder and the ladder collapsed. That *that's* how he died.

CHARLES. By Hauptmann's hand.

REPORTER. But this raises a curious train of logic: In criminal circles, it's commonly known that it takes at least *two* to pull off a kidnapping. One watches after the baby; one does the business dealings and collects the ransom. Plus, think about it: Could Hauptmann really have acted all alone? Why would he have tried to carry the baby down the ladder by himself? There must've been someone else in cahoots. To hold the ladder, at least. It only goes to figure.

CHARLES. I disagree. I was there.

REPORTER. These are the kind of rumors I'm hearing. There's also talk that Hauptmann was the fall guy. That your *wife* did the deadly deed.

CHARLES. Oh, that's ridiculous...

REPORTER. Word is, little Charley wasn't progressing as well as he might have.

CHARLES. Jesus! My son was perfectly normal.

REPORTER. Talk is, he was... you know... *(then)* Slow.

CHARLES. Damn you!

REPORTER. And that your wife... well, you get my drift...

CHARLES. HOW DARE YOU!

REPORTER. I'm just telling you what I hear. *(then)* I've also heard rumors about *you*, Charles.

CHARLES. Me?

REPORTER. They say you never even flew to Paris.

CHARLES. Are you mad? Thousands at Le Bourget saw me land! THERE ARE NEWSREELS!

REPORTER. They say you have an identical twin. That one of you landed in Newfoundland, where the other hopped in and finished the flight.

CHARLES. *(in an utter rage)* I FLEW TO PARIS! I GOD-DAMNED FLEW TO PARIS!

REPORTER. A good reporter hears these things...

CHARLES. Why are you doing this to me?

REPORTER. Come on, Charles.

CHARLES. My son has been murdered! SLAUGHTERED! And it's because of you! YOU did this!

REPORTER. I hardly think...

CHARLES. YOU TOOK MY SON FROM ME!

REPORTER. I'm merely a messenger. An opinionless jerk with a freshly sharpened pencil.

CHARLES. YOU KILLED HIM!

REPORTER. Charles, please —

CHARLES. YOU! KILLED! ME! *(CHARLES begins to cry.)* My only son — my namesake! — has been taken from me. From Anne. And why? BECAUSE WHORES LIKE YOU CONVINCED ME TO TALK WHEN I SHOULD'VE SAID NOTHING! I never wanted to tell my story to *The New York Times*. I hate *The New York Times*! I never wanted to have some pseudo-first-person piece that YOU PEOPLE wrote for me! I spit on you! I PRAY YOU BURN BECAUSE OF THIS! MY SON IS DEAD BECAUSE OF YOU!!

(He weeps. A moment. Then, realizing what he's done, he stops and pulls himself together. A beat.)

REPORTER. *(quiet)* You wanted to be an inventor.

CHARLES. I, um... I'd best be going...

REPORTER. You said you wanted to do this research business, and now I'm told you're getting meetings with some of the country's top scientists.

CHARLES. *(proud)* That's right...

REPORTER. To talk about your goddamned ideal anatomy.

CHARLES. I'm asking questions, trying to learn...

REPORTER. *(over)* Do you have any *idea* how impossible it is to get high-level meetings at the Rockefeller Institute? Columbia University? You never even took biology in college.

CHARLES. *(through clenched teeth)* This is correct.

REPORTER. Why should these scientists waste their precious research time sitting around chatting with *you*?

CHARLES. Because I have fresh ideas.

REPORTER. Do you have even the slightest conception of what the odds are of getting the *full attention* of the Columbia School of Medicine? Can you even conceive how lucky you are?

CHARLES. I have many experiments, so many possibilities in my brain...

REPORTER. Millions of people scribble in their secret journals late at night. Millions harbor these dreams.

CHARLES. Yes, but... *(shouts, a burst of frustration) I'M CHARLES LINDBERGH!!*

(Slight pause)

REPORTER. Of course you are.

ANNE. What should we do with this, Charles?

(Suddenly, ANNE is there, holding a small baby's sun suit with an American flag on the chest.

The REPORTER goes.

ANNE and CHARLES kneel center stage as a pool of light isolates them.)

CHARLES. Oh, I don't...

ANNE. I thought Betty and I had packed away all of his things, but I just found this. Betty let it soak after that afternoon Charley wore it — Lord, when was that? She must've stuck it on a shelf in the laundry room and forgotten to put it away.

Do you remember that afternoon?

CHARLES. *(faint smile)* Yes...

ANNE. It was a Sunday. Or a Saturday?

CHARLES. It was a Sunday. I was holed up in the den.

ANNE. Right, sipping cocoa; it was frightfully cold out.

CHARLES. And you brought him in, dressed in this silly little outfit. More appropriate for the Fourth of July, really, but he did look swell...

ANNE. A summer's day in February. We were playing with him.

CHARLES. Bouncing him up and down. A bit too hard perhaps.

ANNE. Well, yes, because he...

CHARLES. *(with a smile)* Right...

ANNE. And we sat there frozen, not quite sure what to do. He hadn't done that since he was an infant!

CHARLES. It was, well...

ANNE. *(can't help laughing a little)* Do you remember your response? You said something like...

CHARLES. "For God's sake, son, have some respect! You're spitting up all over the American flag!"

(They laugh. A pause.)

ANNE. *(starting to cry)* The poor thing...

CHARLES. *(steeling her)* We can't.

ANNE. I was convinced he had a stomach bug.

(Silence. CHARLES studies the sun suit.)

CHARLES. He looked very handsome in this, you know.

ANNE. Yes.

CHARLES. I'm sure he would've outgrown it by summer. He never could've worn it outside.

ANNE. Yes.

CHARLES. That was a nice afternoon, Anne.

ANNE. Yes.

(A long pause. CHARLES sets the sun suit on the ground between

them. He smoothes it with care. They gaze at it.
Stillness.
Slowly, the lights fade on the two of them, a special light favoring the sun suit so that it's the last thing we see — a tiny American flag amid a vast field of darkness.
Then, the REPORTER enters, watching them from the shadows.
Suddenly, there is a vast EXPLOSION of flashbulbs from all around the stage — POP! POP! POP! But before we can even process this —
Blackout.)

END OF ACT ONE

ACT TWO

"And so Charles had his albatross"

(In darkness, a musical tone. It builds into a chord and keeps building.)

TITLE PROJECTION: **WHERE IS CHARLES LINDBERGH?**

(Suddenly, a pin spot finds the REPORTER, alone. He wears a fedora and speaks into a microphone on a stand, à la Walter Winchell. He's not literally Winchell, just a suggestion of that journalistic type.
Music underscores the following:)

REPORTER. *(into mic)* It's the question on everyone's lips. The house where the kidnapping happened? They no longer live there. Charles' office in the city? Hasn't been there in weeks. The shop on the corner where he gets his leather lace-ups buffed?

Shoe-Shine Johnny tells me he's gone Mexico way. But the *truth*? Ah, the truth. Now, that's anyone's guess.

(Lights up on three FANS.)

FIRST FAN. I saw him at a vegetable stand.

SECOND FAN. I saw him at an airfield.

THIRD FAN. I saw him at a wedding.

REPORTER. *(to the THIRD FAN)* You did?

THIRD FAN. *(sheepish)* Well, I read about it in the paper.

FIRST FAN. *(admits)* Also, I'm not entirely sure it was *him* by the bin of tomatoes. But it could have been; it looked like him.

(The FANS go. A shaft of light isolates the REPORTER.)

REPORTER. *(still into mic, out)* But he really *was* at that airfield, dear listeners. My sources verify this. He was testing a new design — an all-metal Northrop monoplane. But what's this *new* rumor I'm hearing that Lindy's been hiding in plain sight? That he and his wife are in seclusion at their *other* home at Next Day Hill, overcome with grief and unable to leave? I'm not confirming, I'm just suggesting. *(wicked smile)* And let's keep this *entre nous.*

But now a word from our sponsor, Ooh La La Perfume — for the girl who knows romance… just takes a splash of France.

ANNE. Charles, these pages are fine!

(At once, ANNE and CHARLES are there. She's holding several pages of a manuscript.
The music stops. The REPORTER goes.)

CHARLES. *(dismayed)* And you're happy to settle for fine?

ANNE. That's not how I mean it…

CHARLES. Let me go through them once more. I'm certain with some really ruthless editing this time, your article could be much stronger.

ANNE. This is due at *National Geographic* within the week! I still haven't found the ending! I'm never going to finish it if you keep badgering me over every single semicolon!

CHARLES. I'm not *badgering* you, Anne. I'm simply trying to make your prose as solid as it can be.

ANNE. No, you're *trying* to find another excuse to avoid leaving the house at all! *(then, lower)* You haven't left the house in days now.

CHARLES. That's not true.

ANNE. It is…

CHARLES. Please, I went to the bakery, what, just yesterday?

ANNE. You sat in the *car*! You sent Mary in and didn't even go inside. That doesn't count.

CHARLES. Oh, Anne...

ANNE. You need to go out into the world.

CHARLES. Really? Well, I'm not so sure I like this "world" much anymore.

ANNE. What is that supposed to mean?

CHARLES. It means... I'm not sure how comfortable I am living here now.

ANNE. Don't say that.

CHARLES. But it's how I feel.

ANNE. It's far too soon to give even a moment's thought to anything so momentous.

CHARLES. I'm not so sure.

ANNE. Start smaller. Much smaller. Go outside again. Go

for a walk. *(then)* Start there.

CARREL. Charles Lindbergh! To what do I owe the honor?

(At once, ALEXIS CARREL is there. A Frenchman of origin, he's short, stocky and wears thick glasses. He's in his late 50s, though this can be handled theatrically if the actor playing him is much younger.

ACTOR FIVE and ACTOR SIX are in the background, as research assistants.)

TITLE PROJECTION: **TWO WEEKS LATER: THE ROCKEFELLER INSTITUTE, NEW YORK CITY**

CHARLES. Dr. Carrel...

CARREL. Come in!

CHARLES. Thank you for taking the time to see me.

CARREL. Please, I'm a very busy man, but when Charles Lindbergh calls, you put him on your calendar.

CHARLES. Well...

CARREL. So Flagg said something at a party.

CHARLES. Dr. Flagg…

CARREL. At a dinner, yes. He said you wanted to meet with me.

CHARLES. That's right.

CARREL. He was vague as to the why. A few days later, he made a phone call *vouching* for you — for *you*! In a million years, I couldn't imagine what would bring the great aviator into my office!

CHARLES. I'm interested in the mechanical heart.

(A beat)

CARREL. I'm suddenly very intrigued...

CHARLES. One of my wife's sisters has heart disease. There are lesions growing at a very rapid pace, and an operation is an impossibility. First, I thought... well, if there were some way to keep her blood flowing *artificially* while they operated on her heart...

CARREL. Please go on.

CHARLES. *(more roused as he goes)* I mean, the heart is essentially a pump, yes?

CARREL. Well; I suppose —

CHARLES. But then it occurred to me... what if I could devise *more* than a pump, but an actual mechanical heart, which could be placed *inside* a person's chest — permanently even! Can you imagine?

CARREL. *(gentle)* It's a little more complex than you make it out to be.

CHARLES. Yes. Of course.

CARREL. There are bacteria and infections that could cause problems.

CHARLES. Right.

CARREL. Whenever you're dealing with living blood, that raises all kinds of issues. It's not *just* about engineering.

CHARLES. Indeed...

CARREL. But what gives me pause, what stuns and, and *fascinates* me…

Is I've been doing work in this very regard for months now.

CHARLES. *(amazed)* You have...

CARREL. Trying to build a perfusion pump. Which is essentially what you're talking about.

CHARLES. *Really...*

CARREL. An aseptic perfusion pump.

CHARLES. That's... are you serious?

CARREL. Did Flagg say something?

CHARLES. No, no, no —

CARREL. I mean, it's no *secret,* my work. But this *is* a rather remarkable coincidence.

CHARLES. Dr. Carrel, I had no idea —

CARREL. I've spent the last nine months working on this project — nine very grueling, and I don't mind adding very *frustrating* months. I even brought a fellow over from Berlin to help me for a bit — an aeronautical engineer. And a flier like yourself, actually.

CHARLES. Is that so...

CARREL. In theory, my pump should function brilliantly. In *practice...* I'm afraid it hasn't. Infections, as I said.

This is a very tough endeavor you've decided to tackle, Charles Lindbergh.

(A beat)

CHARLES. I can help you.

CARREL. Excuse me?

CHARLES. I'm a flier — just like your man from Berlin — and I know aeronautics. I can help you fix your perfusion pump. I can help you figure out whatever's wrong.

CARREL. My good man — and please don't take this the wrong way — but there is the problem of your practical experience. Or lack thereof, I should say.

CHARLES. I have more experience than you'd think, Dr.

Carrel. These are matters I've been exploring on my own for months, *years* now, actually.

CARREL. But why would someone of your... why would *you* want to involve yourself in anything like this in the first place?

CHARLES. Because this is *precisely* where I want to focus my attentions now!

CARREL. But you hardly even *leave your home* anymore! In the press... please, in the press, they're saying you've become nothing short of a recluse!

CHARLES. *(his hackles up)* You shouldn't believe everything you read in the press! I haven't spoken to them in ages, and I'm a better man for it.

CARREL. And then there is the matter of *my* reputation. *(off CHARLES' look)* Which is questionable. Which is looked about in academia with raised eyebrows at best. *(then)* They say I'm unorthodox.

CHARLES. I've heard these rumblings.

CARREL. They've called me medieval.

CHARLES. Yes, I've read *your* press as well.

CARREL. I'm not sure it would be entirely beneficial for you to associate yourself with someone like me.

(A beat)

CHARLES. Doctor Carrel, after what happened with my son... what I need now are *answers*.

I'm all yours, sir. *(then)* If you want me.

(A beat)

CARREL. So in Charles Lindbergh, I get more than a hero. I

also get a dreamer. *(then)* This I like. This I like very much.

(A musical chord. The REPORTER appears in a shaft of light, again in Walter Winchell mode. As before, he speaks into a mic on a stand.
CHARLES and CARREL go.)

REPORTER. Charles Lindbergh getting cozy with a dicey academic? Strange as it may sound, my sources tell me this is true. Is the ace flyer swapping his goggles for a microscope? I'm not confirming, I'm just suggesting. *(wicked smile)* And let's keep this *entre nous*.

(shifting quickly) Oh my God, you're Charles Lindbergh!

(The REPORTER suddenly turns to CHARLES; he has dropped his Walter Winchell guise.)

TITLE PROJECTION: **AT JOSLIN'S MARKET**

CHARLES. *(unsure of the connection)* Yes... hello...

REPORTER. I cannot believe Charles Lindbergh does his own shopping!

CHARLES. Do I... I'm sorry, do I know you?

REPORTER. Oh, I think you know me. I'm a stringer with the *New York Herald*. I'd love to talk with you for a moment.

CHARLES. *(abrupt, his guard up suddenly)* I'm afraid that won't be possible.

REPORTER. So what's this science business all about?

CHARLES. Please leave me alone...

REPORTER. What do you hope to accomplish at the Rockefeller Institute — where I hear you've now got a *full research post*? Very impressive.

CHARLES. This conversation is ending. Right now. *Go.*

REPORTER. Charles, tell me what you're working on! I want to know!

CHARLES. I'm a very busy man —

REPORTER. Doing what, *buying eggs*?

CHARLES. Yes, *buying eggs*! Leave me alone!

REPORTER. And what's this I hear that there's *another* Lindbergh baby now?

(A little beat)

CHARLES. *(stops, deeply shaken at that)* Pardon me...?

REPORTER. A little boy? Named Jonathan, is it? And growing up so fast? Already older than your *first* one was when that poor kid was, well, y'know —

CHARLES. *(a few inches from his face)* YOU DO NOT WRITE ABOUT JONATHAN! YOU DO NOT TALK TO ME! DO YOU UNDERSTAND? YOU STAY THE HELL AWAY FROM MY FAMILY AND JUST....! *(pulling himself together, then)* Let me buy my eggs.

ANNE. But certainly that's not worth leaving *our home* over!

(Suddenly, ANNE is there. We're back at the Lindbergh home at Next Day Hill.
The REPORTER goes.)

CHARLES. It *is*, Anne. Don't you see? They linger in the

hedges, waiting to pounce whenever they can.

ANNE. You're making too much of this.

CHARLES. Am I? Every day, it seems, I open the paper and see these stories about the kidnapping — *(Corrects himself:)* The *murder*. And then with the trial and the investigation and the public's *fascination* with the whole matter… I think it's best if we just leave.

ANNE. I hate to think *that's* the only option…

CHARLES. But it is. My God, with everything that's happened. And with Jonathan now. We cannot raise another child here.

ANNE. Oh, Charles...

CHARLES. You know I'm right.

(A beat)

ANNE. *(a little lost)* But where would we go...?

CHARLES. I've inquired about an estate in Kent.

ANNE. *(laughs at the absurdity of that)* Kent? And I'm sorry, an *estate*?!

CHARLES. *(laughs at that too)* It's not as grand as it sounds...

ANNE. So you've been inquiring, have you?

CHARLES. I've asked around.

ANNE. I don't believe this!

CHARLES. *(conspiratorially)* It's on this enormous piece of property — acres! — with character to spare. You'd love it there.

ANNE. I'm sorry, you want to move us to the British countryside just like that? You want us to abandon America entirely?

CHARLES. I've entertained the thought...

ANNE. But you've just started working with Dr. Carrel.

CHARLES. Yes, that's —

ANNE. So now you're, what, you're going to *break off* all your ties with him?

CHARLES. I have no intention of breaking off anything! We've worked together intensely for the last five months. I think it would be fine if we worked independently for a while. *(with a little smile)* And they have these little things called *airplanes* now.

(A little beat)

ANNE. I don't know what to say to any of this.

CHARLES. Say yes. I need to escape for a little bit. We all do.

ANNE. I realize that, but —

CHARLES. I just need to get *away*. From the world. From society. And from the revolting press as well.

(POP! POP! POP! Flashes explode. The REPORTER is isolated in a pool of light.)

TITLE PROJECTION: **FROM THE PAGES OF THE *NEW YORK DAILY NEWS***

REPORTER. *(out, without the Winchell persona)* "Somehow in the course of events, Charles Lindbergh has decided he's Greta Garbo. The fact is, he would have been pestered less if he had acted more as a popular hero is supposed to act."

CARREL. *(stunned)* You're moving into a fourteenth-century estate in *Kent*?!

(At once, CARREL is there. The REPORTER and ANNE go.)

CARREL. You're from Minnesota! The Duchess of Windsor is from Baltimore! I sincerely hope you can appreciate the bizarre similarity.

CHARLES. So I'll go. I'll be Greta Garbo.

CARREL. In England, no doubt.

CHARLES. It'll be wonderful. I'll play with my son. Fly around, explore Europe.

CARREL. *(considers)* Europe *could* be a good environment for our research.

CHARLES. And the best part?

CARREL. Yes?

CHARLES. I can continue our work with even more vigor.

(A musical chord. The REPORTER is there. CARREL goes. CHARLES lingers.)

REPORTER. *(into mic, a la Winchell)* Charles Lindbergh publishing articles about *chloroformed cats* in the pages of *Science Magazine*? What is the world coming to, dear listeners? And what exactly *does* he hope to accomplish in his asylum in his estate in Kent? I'm not confirming, I'm just suggesting. And let's keep this *entre nous*.

ANNE. I am here to save Octavius from an imminent death!

(The lights shift. ANNE is there. We're in a musty barn on the Lindbergh's estate in Kent. CHARLES consults a massive book. By his side is a small cage. The REPORTER goes.)

CHARLES. Octavius...?

ANNE. The rat. Your victim. Jon and I have already named him.

CHARLES. Oh, for God's sake.

ANNE. I'm serious. His little animals keep disappearing; he worries. You're giving him an abandonment complex, Charles.

CHARLES. I'm studying hypothermia.

ANNE. On the family pets.

CHARLES. On rats!

ANNE. Very cute, very clean rats. Almost-like-guinea-pig rats. To our two-year-old son, they're little dogs. I'm afraid you're murdering puppies, dear.

CHARLES. I'm studying lowered bodily temperatures.

ANNE. Try explaining that to a child. *(then)* So how's this all coming?

CHARLES. Oh... wonderfully! It's fascinating how the body responds to radically lowered temperatures. Slows everything right down with no damage whatsoever, far as I can tell.

ANNE. But what are you really doing out here in a *barn* on a beautiful Saturday afternoon?

CHARLES. Excuse me?

ANNE. It's... well, I'm curious. What's the grand scheme?

CHARLES. I don't know... I think maybe something momentous...

ANNE. Is that so?

CHARLES. I think maybe perfection.

ANNE. *(a little uneasy)* Really...

CHARLES. I think... I think I might actually be building a better man.

(A beat)

ANNE. *(her guard up now)* Are you serious...?

CHARLES. I am...

ANNE. This is... "Frankenstein." Listen to yourself!

CHARLES. Hear me out, Anne. In this pump we've designed, we've been able to keep animals' organs alive outside the body — on their own, free of infection — for more than two weeks! Spleens, ovaries, hearts! And all of this — and Carrel agrees with me — all of this points in one direction. We could create a better human *being*. A *perfect* human being!

(A beat)

ANNE. Are you happy here, Charles?

CHARLES. Am I... [happy]? Anne, I'm happier than I've been in years! I can work uninterrupted. We can fly here and there, no worries whatsoever.

ANNE. Yes, that's...

CHARLES. And I'm *meeting* all kinds of people; intelligent people. People who can further my research. Like the Germans I've met.

ANNE. *(a little taken aback at that)* Is that so…?

CHARLES. On my last two trips, I've come in contact with some very bright men who seem... Well, Germany *does* seem to be the most interesting country in the world right now.

ANNE. You think that?

CHARLES. I do.

ANNE. The Nazis are far too fanatical for my taste.

CHARLES. But their *ideas… are* intriguing. Their aviation facilities, their architecture, the condition of the country itself.

ANNE. *(uncomfortable)* So on these trips... you've met

Nazis who intrigue you?

CHARLES. Anne, the German people I've met have been uniformly hard-working and clear-eyed... *science*-minded. They could help me — us — Carrel and I.

ANNE. I worry sometimes that things are moving too fast now...

CHARLES. What are you talking about?

ANNE. You just... you jump to these conclusions out here in our barn. About your work, about *perfection* —

CHARLES. Moving too *fast*? I feel like things are moving too *slow* —

ANNE. Then you go off, you meet these people —

CHARLES. I have all of this time, this freedom now...

ANNE. I can see that...

CHARLES. No one's looking over my shoulder!

ANNE. Still, I worry. I worry quite a bit.

CHARLES. But there's *nothing* to worry about. Our life here is wonderful! *Europe* is wonderful! *(then, with a little smile)* Please, I don't even mind going out in public anymore.

GÖRING. *Herr Lindbergh!*

(HERMANN GÖRING appears. We're at a dinner party. Light music plays.

GÖRING is a blustery heavyset man, wearing crisp dinner clothes. Again, this can be handled theatrically. GÖRING holds a small red box and makes a beeline to CHARLES.)

TITLE PROJECTION: **AT THE HOME OF THE AMERICAN AMBASSADOR TO GERMANY. BERLIN, 1937**

CHARLES. Yes...?

GÖRING. *Ich habe die ungewoehnliche Ehre, ihnen den Orden des Deutschen Adlers im Namen des Deutschen Reiches zu Überreichen.*

(From the box, he removes a Service Cross, which is hung upon a thin ribbon. He places this around CHARLES' neck. Awkward pause.)

CHARLES. I don't know what to say... I don't speak any German.

(At once, a female TRANSLATOR is there.)

TRANSLATOR. Reichsmarschall Göring says that he...

CHARLES. *(overlapping)* Göring?

TRANSLATOR. This is Reichsmarschall Hermann Göring. And he says that he wishes to present you with the Order of the German Eagle. By special proclamation of the Third Reich.

GÖRING. *Dieser Orden ist das zweithöchste Deutsche Ehrenzeichen.*

TRANSLATOR. He says that this is the second highest of all German decorations.

GÖRING. *Es Ehrt diejenigen ausländischen Männer, die vom Reich bwundort werden.*

TRANSLATOR. It honors foreign men who have done well of the Reich.

GÖRING. *Er ist ihnen auf Befehl des Führers verliehen worden.*

TRANSLATOR. And it has been bestowed upon you by order of the Fuehrer.

CHARLES. The *Fuehrer...?*

PRESS REPRESENTATIVE. Pardon me, Marshal Göring.

(A PRESS REPRESENTATIVE is there.)

PRESS REPRESENTATIVE. I'm from the Ambassador's press office. Colonel Lindbergh is about to sit down to dinner.

ANNE. *(a bit relieved, to the PRESS REPRESENTATIVE)* Yes, hello. Thank you.

PRESS REPRESENTATIVE. *(to the TRANSLATOR)* Kindly ask him if we couldn't do this privately, over brandy perhaps.

(She whispers the translation.)

GÖRING. *(enraged) Verwigert er meinen Orden?*

TRANSLATOR. *Sie missverstehen ihn...*

CHARLES. What's he saying?

TRANSLATOR. Marshal Göring is worried that you're rejecting his country's medal.

CHARLES. Please, tell him that I —

GÖRING. *Bei Gott, das ist eine Beleidigung!*

CHARLES. *(to GÖRING)* On the contrary, sir!

ANNE. Charles! Dear...

CHARLES. *(to GÖRING) Danke schön!*

PRESS REPRESENTATIVE. Sir, we had no idea Göring was planning this ceremony. This was not cleared through our office.

GÖRING. *Ich bin empört!*

ANNE. Charles, I really think we should discuss this, the two of us. This has implications.

CHARLES. What, you're saying I should give this back —

this, this German Eagle, did he say? That's not an option. That isn't done.

ANNE. It's from Hitler. There are issues to consider.

PRESS REPRESENTATIVE. Refusing an award would undoubtedly cause quite a stir. Outside this room, I'm talking now. In the press. We should discuss this later, when the circumstances are more controlled.

CHARLES. I've received loads of these. Nearly two hundred! What's one more?

ANNE. It's late. We ought to ponder this with a clear head.

CHARLES. Henry Ford got a medal from the Germans. It didn't bother him.

ANNE. This one's from *Hitler*...

PRESS REPRESENTATIVE. We shouldn't make any rash decisions here...

CHARLES. It's a fragment of tin! Anne, let's not make more of this than it is. Refusing it would call more attention to it than accepting it quietly like a gentleman. I wouldn't want to create a scene. Actually, that's the last thing I want to do.

(He confers briefly with the TRANSLATOR. Little pause.)

CHARLES. *(clumsily, to GÖRING) Vielen dank.*

(A dramatic lighting shift. Everyone steps forward in a line and speaks out, as if talking to the press.)

PRESS REPRESENTATIVE. And that's how Charles Lindbergh came to be presented with the Order of the German Eagle.

ANNE. *(concerned)* The second highest of all German

honors...

GÖRING. *Auf Befehl des Dritten Reichs.*

TRANSLATOR. From the Fuehrer.

PRESS REPRESENTATIVE. Colonel Lindbergh has a statement. He says, and I quote —

CHARLES. I feel no differently about this particular medal than I do about any other honor I've received from any foreign government. I've always liked the Germans.

GÖRING. *Es war...*

TRANSLATOR. It was...

ANNE. I took one look at that medal and knew it was his albatross.

PRESS REPRESENTATIVE. Mr. Lindbergh would like to add —

CHARLES. A few more months spent in Germany would be interesting from many standpoints. I think I'd like to live here for a while.

ANNE. And that was that.

PRESS REPRESENTATIVE. That's all he has to say.

CHARLES. Good night.

ANNE. Yes. And so Charles had his albatross.

(Suddenly, POP! POP! POP! An EXPLOSION of flashbulbs.)

ICKES. Fellow Americans, I ask you: How is one of our own capable of so unthinking an act?

(HAROLD ICKES, the Secretary of the Interior, appears. Everyone else goes.)

TITLE PROJECTION: **FROM A SPEECH BY HAROLD ICKES, SECRETARY OF THE INTERIOR**

ICKES. *(out)* How can any American accept a decoration at the hand of a brutal dictator who, with that same hand, is robbing and torturing thousands of fellow human beings?

(POP! POP! POP! Another EXPLOSION.)

TITLE PROJECTION: **FROM THE PAGES OF *THE NEW YORKER***

(The REPORTER appears as ICKES goes.)

REPORTER. *(out)* With confused emotions we say good-bye to Colonel Charles A. Lindbergh, who wants to go and live in Berlin, presumably occupying a house that once belonged to Jews. If he wants to experiment further with the artificial heart, his surroundings there should be ideal.

(POP! POP! POP! Another EXPLOSION.)

TITLE PROJECTION: **FROM A STATEMENT BY THE WHITE HOUSE**

(A SPOKESMAN appears as the REPORTER goes.)

SPOKESMAN. *(out)* The news of the past few days from Germany has deeply shocked public opinion in the United States. President Roosevelt himself could scarcely believe that such things could occur in a twentieth century civilization.

(POP! POP! POP! Another EXPLOSION.)

TITLE PROJECTION: **FROM A PRESS RELEASE BY TWA**

(A PRESS AGENT appears as the SPOKESMAN goes.)

PRESS AGENT. *(out, with forced cheer)* Greetings, press corps! Enclosed is our 1939 promotional calendar. You may notice the omission of our longtime slogan, "The Lindbergh Line." This is not in error. We have chosen to discontinue its use and hope you will stop referring to us in this manner. From all of us at TWA, thank you!

(Suddenly, we hear the low, long blast of an ocean liner's whistle.
Blackout.)

TITLE PROJECTION: **ABOARD THE AQUITANIA IN NEW YORK HARBOR**

(We're in a state room on the ocean liner.)

CARREL. My God, Charles — *what are you doing*?!

(CHARLES and CARREL are there.)

CHARLES. *(taken aback at that)* Carrel …?

CARREL. These actions of yours — they're undermining our work!

CHARLES. Please… no… don't make what's happening into something it's not…

CARREL. Something it's *NOT*?! Do you know how many strings I had to pull to *be* here even? To get to you *first*?

CHARLES. *(with a little smirk)* I don't even want to know how you were able to hop on board before we got through customs...

CARREL. My friend, there are throngs of reporters waiting for you *on the dock*! Can you appreciate the magnitude of all this?

CHARLES. I'm sure you're blowing this all out of proportion...

(The REPORTER appears in a special.)

REPORTER. Hiya, Charlie. We can't *wait* to talk to you this time.

(He vanishes.)

CHARLES. Oh my God...!

CARREL. Well, exactly!

(A little beat)

CHARLES. So... so fine, I'm no longer the fair-haired child of the American press. I've never cared about what anyone thought of me anyway.

CARREL. Yes, but even you must realize that there's a vast difference between being left alone and being reviled.

(A beat)

CHARLES. Surely people don't hate me...

CARREL. I dare say you're still regarded as something of a hero; stature like that doesn't vanish overnight. But you've got to be exceedingly careful about what you say next, whom you support.

CHARLES. I wasn't *supporting* anyone —! I accepted a gift, end of story.

CARREL. Charles, you're acquainted with Nazis!

CHARLES. Yes, *acquainted*. That's all.

CARREL. That's enough.

CHARLES. I met them... I'll have you know I *met* them during my trips abroad, which were *funded* by the U.S. government so I could suss out Germany's air facilities! And I can tell you this, Carrel, theirs are far beyond America's in terms of technology and capacity.

CARREL. *(he didn't know this) Really...*

CHARLES. Indeed! And since I don't think we have a prayer on the *ground* either, I don't understand what the whole fuss is about in the first place!

(A little beat)

CARREL. Hold on... so what are you saying here...?

CHARLES. That America doesn't belong in this war!

CARREL. I'm sorry... then you're arguing for…

CHARLES. Neutrality. Right down the line. My dear friend, this is a European squabble. There's no reason why America should step into the fray.

CARREL. *(his hackles up)* But *neutrality*, Charles… how can you just *ignore* what's happening abroad? *(then)* Oh I'm sorry, why do you even care? You've announced you're moving to Berlin! You're practically a German citizen now.

CHARLES. After *Kristallnacht*? I'd have to be a fool.

(Pause)

CARREL. So you're *not* moving?

CHARLES. With the riots and such, I'm afraid not. This isn't the time to set up housekeeping in Germany. Besides, I don't want to give anyone the impression that I approve of what's happened. It's dreadful.

CARREL. *(stunned)* No one stateside knows this.

CHARLES. I don't speak to the press directly.

CARREL. You should tell someone these things. A sympathetic reporter.

CHARLES. No! That would mean starting that vulgar dialogue all over again.

CARREL. You have a conscience and a heart — and realize *Kristallnacht* is unacceptable. Let people know this!

CHARLES . Carrel, if… *if* I were to even *consider* entering public life again, it would have to be on my own terms. In my own *words*.

CARREL. I beg of you, my friend. Please choose them very carefully.

(CARREL goes. CHARLES moves to center where a microphone is placed before him by the REPORTER, who adjusts the cables and makes sure everything is set. As CHARLES dons a set of headphones and consults a speech he pulls from his breast pocket, we hear an announcer.)

RADIO ANNOUNCER. *(V.O.)* From the studios of radio station WOL in our nation's capital comes a rare public statement from Colonel Charles A. Lindbergh. The ever-reclusive Lindbergh has made no such announcement in twelve years...

TITLE PROJECTION: **SEPTEMBER 15, 1939**

(We hear a recording of the actual Lindbergh.)

CHARLES. *(recorded)* These wars in Europe are not wars in which our civilization is defending itself against some Asiatic intruder. There is no Genghis Khan or Xerxes marching against our Western nations.

(The CHARLES onstage begins to speak along with the Charles on tape, until our CHARLES has taken over entirely.)

CHARLES. This is not a question of banding together to defend the white race against foreign invasion. We must not permit our sentiment, our pity, or our personal feelings of sympathy, to obscure the issue. We must be as impersonal as the surgeon with his knife.

(We hear STATIC! It fades out.)

CARREL. Oh, Charles, what have you done?

(At once, CARREL is there. The REPORTER lingers.)

CHARLES. You know how I feel about neutrality.

CARREL. Yes, but there are millions of people who feel that Genghis Khan *is* marching toward them and that his name is Adolph Hitler. Your choice of imagery was thoughtless, at best.

CHARLES. *(angry)* I'm not a coward, Doctor! If we're attacked first, of course we should fight back. I just don't think we ought to provoke anything.

(CARREL goes.

The front page of a tabloid is projected — enormously — along the back wall; it should be as big and shocking as possible. The headline reads: "LINDY LANDS IN MAJOR MESS!"

The REPORTER steps forward. He speaks into a microphone with a banner from "NBC Radio." He has the clipped delivery of a serious, hard-nosed newsman, much less unctuous than his Winchell persona.)

REPORTER. *(into mic)* Colonel Charles Lindbergh has landed back in the public eye, though this time amid great controversy.

COLLEGE STUDENT. Dear Mr. Lindbergh.

(A female COLLEGE STUDENT is there. The projection remains.

Onstage, we're in a sort of theatrical limbo. Various ACTORS appear and stand in a semi-circle around CHARLES, who is center stage.)

COLLEGE STUDENT. I'm a student at Sarah Lawrence College. I would never ordinarily write this sort of letter — I'm a very quiet person. But I feel compelled to tell you that I find it very offensive you mentioned the "white race" in your argument. You've turned the war question into a matter of ethnicity. Just like Hitler. How long were you in Berlin anyway?

REPORTER. Colonel! How do you feel about the growing concern that your radio address was anti-Jewish?

(The REPORTER moves into the scene.)

CHARLES. I never even mentioned the Jews!

REPORTER. No, but Jewish people are suffering mightily in Europe, and you asked our country to turn its back, to feel no sympathy. And that word — "sympathy" — sounds rather condescending, don't you think?

CHARLES. People are interpreting my remarks as anti-Jewish?

REPORTER. Is it true you're being wooed by the Republicans as an opponent to Roosevelt in '40?

SPOKESMAN. *(to the REPORTER)* The White House feels that Lindbergh is shockingly presumptive in posing as an expert in foreign affairs.

(Roosevelt's SPOKESMAN is there.)

SPOKESMAN. The President would remind you that this is a man who has been decorated by the Nazi party. His is hardly an unbiased voice.

CARREL. I hear you're thinking of going on the radio again. Is this true?

(CARREL is there.)

CHARLES. It's something I've considered...

ANNE. I really don't understand this sudden need to speak your mind.

(Now, ANNE is there as well.)

ANNE. You've bitten your tongue for years. Why now?

SPOKESMAN. Lindbergh has a personal agenda.

ANNE. There's no need for you to keep talking.

CHARLES. But I *must* keep talking, Anne. *Especially* now.

ANNE. But why?

CHARLES. I *have* to do whatever I can to keep America from entering this war!

ANNE. Yes, but Charles…

CHARLES. And fine, if I can use my, my... who I am to some good, then that's what I must do.

ANNE. But maybe we shouldn't act so rashly.

CHARLES. What are you saying?

ANNE. Maybe we should step back a bit.

COLLEGE STUDENT. I beg of you, Mr. Lindbergh: Stop speaking of the war in terms of race.

REPORTER. You should talk to me. I only have your best interests in mind.

ANNE. Don't do this.

CHARLES. I hate being a public figure. But this isn't the time to think about myself.

ANNE. Charles. Still…

CHARLES. *America has no business policing the world! (then)* How arrogant is it for us to feel we must? And if people will listen to what I have to say simply because I've achieved some measure of fame — and I hate that word! — then I have no choice but to come forward.

ANNE. But they're misinterpreting your words.

CHARLES. I can change that.

SPOKESMAN. Lindbergh is not one of us.

ANNE. It's best to bow out, Charles.

REPORTER. Lindbergh, please talk to me.

ANNE. You promised me an uneventful life — I'm calling you on that now!

(A beat)

CHARLES. I've agreed to speak in Des Moines.

ANNE. Don't go.

CHARLES. The fight for neutrality needs me.

COLLEGE STUDENT. Mr. Lindbergh, please hear the plea of a college student who had to *force* herself to write this letter.

CARREL. Consider our future.

ANNE. Consider our children.

CHARLES. Anne, if people will listen, they'll know I'm only trying to reason with them.

CARREL. Lindbergh...

ANNE. You talk of race in such specific terms —

CHARLES. *Scientific.* A Jew is a Jew.

REPORTER. Lindbergh!

ANNE. You see it as exactitude. Most people see that kind of labeling as bigotry.

CHARLES. I'm trying to be *precise*. No room for error.

SPOKESMAN. *(shaking his head in dismay)* Lindbergh...

ANNE. You're flying in circles and don't even realize it.

CARREL. *(begging)* Lindbergh...

CHARLES. It's important to be exact. It's important to state my case with utter clarity.

CARREL / ROOSEVELT / REPORTER / COLLEGE STUDENT. *LINDBERGH!!!*

(ALL go, except for ANNE and CHARLES. The projection of the tabloid fades.)

ANNE. *(producing a few typewritten pages)* You cannot say this!

TITLE PROJECTION: **AT THE LINDBERGH HOME, IN HIDING ON MARTHA'S VINEYARD**

CHARLES. I can say whatever I like.

ANNE. Charles, do you really believe these words?

CHARLES. I do. Of course, I do.

ANNE. Because they're positively… Your supporters — the America First people? — I really can't expect they're going to agree with you.

CHARLES. Then they're not my true supporters, are they?

ANNE. You must realize the *reaction* this will have! I'm sick to think of it.

CHARLES. I've never been so sure of anything in my life.

ANNE. You'll say these words, and people will instantly

think the worst of you.

CHARLES. You're overreacting.

ANNE. But don't you see? They won't be able to hear your message because the *way you're saying it* is so damnable! *(off the pages in her hand)* This isn't you. You should start off by saying, "I'm not anti-Semitic." I can rewrite this for you.

CHARLES. *(terse)* I don't need you to do that.

ANNE. Then I'm going to tear this up.

CHARLES. Now you're being childish.

ANNE. I'm going to burn it so you won't say these things!

CHARLES. Give me back the speech.

ANNE. *(frantically, calling off)* Mary, do we have any matches?

CHARLES. Anne…

ANNE. I'm going to do this...

CHARLES. Stop this…

ANNE. Mary! Are you there, Mary?!

CHARLES. Can I be any clearer? GIVE ME THE SPEECH!!!

(A pause. She does so.)

ANNE. *(quiet)* I never dreamed anything could make me question my affection for you.

CHARLES. Oh, for God's sake, Anne. Let me make my case in, what, a *handful* of pages?

ANNE. Pages filled with incendiary words!

CHARLES. That I hope will start a *dialogue! (angry)* And now you're saying you hate me? Is this right? What, you're going to *leave* me because of some little talk?

ANNE. Your mind is made up, then. You're giving the speech?

(He says nothing. She turns to go, but stops short.)

ANNE. You are my husband, Charles Lindbergh. Of course I don't hate you. This does, however, make me doubt my love for you.

(She goes. We hear a recording the actual Lindbergh, speaking at a rally. CHARLES faces forward, silent, the real Charles speaking for him at first.)

CHARLES. *(recorded)* We cannot allow the natural passions and prejudices of other peoples to lead our country to destruction. *(LOUD CROWD BOO)* Its members have used... *(CROWD BOO)* Its members have used the war emergency...

TITLE PROJECTION: **THE AMERICA FIRST RALLY: DES MOINES, SEPTEMBER 11, 1941**

(CHARLES begins speaking along with the recording, but soon it is only CHARLES that we hear. The "boos" continue under.)

CHARLES. *(more impassioned as he goes)* Instead of agitating for war, the Jewish groups in this country should be opposing it in every possible way, for they will be among the first to feel its consequences. The Jewish people's greatest danger to this country lies in their ownership and influence in our motion pictures, our press, our radio, and our government.

(In darkness: POP! POP! POP! Then lights up fast and blind-

ingly bright. The other actors run in, quickly and aggressively, making their anger palpable.

CHARLES moves far downstage, feeling the assault of their words. Very fast:)

REPORTER. So now you're calling the Jews *war-mongers*?

COLLEGE STUDENT. Dear Mr. Lindbergh — your latest speech fills me with such utter *despair*!

SPOKESMAN. Lindbergh's words of late have been debatable at best, but these comments reflect a plotting that smells rancidly of Hitler.

CARREL. My friend, I fear you've made a grave error.

CHARLES. *(very upset at the reaction he's caused)* But no... *no*... I'm just trying to say what I believe!

ANNE. Believe in silence, Charles.

REPORTER. An editorial: "This is the most un-American talk made in our time by any person of national reputation."

SPOKESMAN. How tragic that one of our nation's most beloved heroes would turn against us.

CHARLES. *(to ANNE)* Don't get me wrong, I admire the Jews! Jews of a right type are an asset to *any* country.

ANNE. Charles! You need to stop speaking! Now!

CARREL. I'm afraid I must disassociate myself from our work.

SPOKESMAN. The White House believes it would be best for all of us if Lindbergh would simply go away.

CARREL. I hereby grant you all of our research.

REPORTER. I have no more questions.

CHARLES. Carrel, I want to keep working together...

CARREL. And that's where we differ. I don't.

SPOKESMAN. And so we move on to more important matters.

REPORTER. And so —

COLLEGE STUDENT. And so I turn my attention back to my studies, Mr. Lindbergh. *(then)* And sadly, away from you.

(As one, the other ACTORS fall away.

The light flickers — then, blackness all around the stage, except for CHARLES in his "airplane" again in a shaft of blinding light. Rushing wind. Eerie peace. CHARLES tries to bask in this moment, but he's troubled, agitated. It doesn't work this time. He grows increasingly frustrated.

At once, the lights shift back — and only the REPORTER is there. He's a more world-weary, worldly wise version of the man we met in Paris.)

CHARLES. *(utterly lost)* May I... may I talk to you...?

REPORTER. What?

CHARLES. Could we...? I was… Could we start over.

REPORTER. I don't understand...

CHARLES. I need to talk to someone. Please. I'm afraid I might say the wrong thing, and I... well, I thought...

REPORTER. That I might help you.

CHARLES. I hoped so.

REPORTER. And what did you want to talk about?

CHARLES. I was... well, I was hoping you might help me put things right.

REPORTER. I see.

CHARLES. I was hoping you might help me be *clear*. Clearer than I've been.

REPORTER. By telling people *what* exactly?

CHARLES. Well… my *views*… only in ways that people can understand them.

REPORTER. I'm sorry, but that won't be possible.

CHARLES. Just a few minutes is all I'm asking —

REPORTER. I'm a very busy man —

CHARLES. For years, for*ever* you people have been begging me to talk, and now I'm... don't you see? I'm finally willing to do that! On *your terms* even —

REPORTER. I really need to get going.

CHARLES. All I want is a few *minutes* —

REPORTER. I have other stories to pursue —

CHARLES. *(a bit desperate)* Do you know about television?

(A little beat)

REPORTER. Sorry?

CHARLES. This invention, they showed it at the World's Fair.

REPORTER. Yes...?

CHARLES. The Germans have had it for years. They broadcast the Olympics in '36.

REPORTER. I should go...

CHARLES. Because I was thinking, if television were more advanced in this country — right now, say — it could help me tell my story the way it should be told.

REPORTER. It's too late...

CHARLES. No! We could talk and our words would be spat into America's homes instantaneously; it would be so *exact.*

REPORTER. I don't think so...

CHARLES. Charles Lindbergh, live in your home! It will be the scoop of the decade.

REPORTER. But no one would want to watch that.

(A beat)

CHARLES. How can you say that...?

REPORTER. Because.... please... No one cares about you anymore.

CHARLES. *(getting angry now)* That... that is *untrue*... and completely insulting!

REPORTER. *(getting angry himself)* You have committed... for God's sake, Charles, you have done this *terrible* act with what you've said!

CHARLES. You're exaggerating immensely...

REPORTER. Trust me, I'm not!

CHARLES. Did I... I'm sorry, did I *harm* anyone?!

REPORTER. Some would say you had.

CHARLES. Oh, come on now —

REPORTER. Some would say your attack is just as vicious as any —

CHARLES. *(over)* My *attack*...? Words! Ideas! We're talking about *WORDS* here!

REPORTER. Every bit as hateful!

CHARLES. Words don't have the power to *destroy*!

REPORTER. Of course they do!

CHARLES. I only said what I believed —

REPORTER. And destroyed *YOURSELF*!

(A little beat)

REPORTER. Charles, my God — *(then, an EXPLOSION that builds)* You have gone from being our country's most beloved hero to its most despised citizen in a matter of FOURTEEN YEARS! And by doing NOTHING that even comes *CLOSE* to a federal offense! CAN YOU *FATHOM* HOW DIFFICULT THAT IS?! *YOU HAVE BECOME FATTY ARBUCKLE*!! *(then)* And for that… *(low, bitter)* I pity you very much.

(The REPORTER starts to go.)

CHARLES. *(spent, wounded)* No, no, wait... I want to say something...

(The REPORTER hesitates.)

CHARLES. *(struggles to put this into words)* I want to get this right now... and *on the record*. I would like... I would like to say —

BETTY. Colonel, have you got the baby? Don't fool with me; he needs his sleep.

(Suddenly, one by one, the other ACTORS begin appearing.)

ANNE. Charles, please tell me this is another of your awful jokes!

CHARLES. *(turns to them, a bit disoriented)* The baby? Has something happened to the baby...?

POLICE DETECTIVE. Start from the beginning.

PHOTOGRAPHER. Give us a weepy mug, okay?

(At once, they fall away, leaving ANNE and CHARLES in a cove of light at center. The REPORTER lingers.)

ANNE. Who would do this, Charles?! Why would anyone want to take our *child* away from us?

CHARLES. I'm, I'm struggling to find some explanation...

ANNE. This afternoon, we had a family. Tonight, our son... our *family* is gone!

CHARLES. This all must be some gross misunderstanding.

ANNE. I feel so lost, Charles.

CHARLES. Yes...

ANNE. I feel like part of me is already gone.

CHARLES. Yes...

ANNE. And I'm supposed to live forty, fifty, sixty more years even? That seems utterly impossible.

CHARLES. I think the best thing... I think the best thing right now would be if we said a little prayer for baby Charley.

ANNE. I think... that sounds like a beautiful idea.

(They join hands.)

CHARLES. I pray for you, my son.

ANNE. I pray that you're in considerate hands tonight.

CHARLES. I pray for your safety.

ANNE. I pray that you'll be back with us very soon.

CHARLES. And Charley, I'm just... *(with tremendous anguish)* I'm so sorry.

(ANNE goes. CHARLES turns back to face the REPORTER.)

CHARLES. What I'm trying to say here is… I'm just so…

(A very long beat. He can't say the words.)

REPORTER. Goodbye, Charles.

(The REPORTER goes, leaving CHARLES alone. A brief news-

reel of the "real" Charles Lindbergh early in his life, perhaps from '27, is projected at rear, filling the entire back wall. There is no sound. CHARLES stands in silhouette alone against the screen, as the "Charles" on the film smiles and waves. This footage would preferably be pre-kidnapping.

And then, quite suddenly, the film breaks — a very jarring effect. We are left with a brightly lit, blank screen at rear, and utter, stunning silence. CHARLES stands there, exposed in harsh, white light. The lights fade on him. He goes.

Then, ANNE reappears. She moves into a cove of light.)

ANNE. *(out)* When the war came, Charles did his part. He flew as a fighter pilot, throughout the Pacific and under an alias. You can imagine what a coup it would have been for the Japanese to shoot down the great Charles Lindbergh!

He didn't have to see combat. He volunteered.

Many people have asked me how *I* felt about what Charles said and about the way things played out.

You want to say, "He's not a bad person." You want to say, "If you'd only been there, you would understand why he *thought* he was doing the right thing." But that sounds like a defense. And so I say nothing.

During periods of trouble, sadness... I often think back to the time when I first fell in love with Charles. He had come for a week to visit our family in Mexico City — just seven months after the Paris flight! I was so young, and he was... well, he was the most breathtaking man I'd ever seen. So heroic. That whole week, I found myself at an embarrassing loss for words whenever I was in his presence — stammering, stumbling, saying nothing of any worth. When I found myself seated next to him at a lunch one afternoon, I became so tongue-tied I finally gave up and stopped talking altogether — said absolutely nothing at all!

I discovered later that Charles loved silence. That *that lunch* was the first time he'd ever felt at home with a girl.

It's funny... much of my life with Charles has been about silence. Solitude. About being in the back cockpit. About being home with the children while he's off exploring the world. About being home alone, while he's off in Germany, where he seems to be more and more these days. About feeling so alone, so lost, so *angry* even... wondering whether this should have been my journey at all.

Solitude...

(A beat; she brightens a bit.)

ANNE. But today Charles is off on yet another adventure.

(CHARLES appears, wearing a loosely knotted tie and holding a jacket, which he slips into.)

CHARLES. Right, where am I headed this time?

ANNE. *(still out)* After the war, Charles was on a team of experts who traveled all over Germany. Touring aircraft factories that had been dismantled, talking with aeronautical engineers; it was invigorating work. *(turning to him, tightening his tie for him)* See, you should wear a nice tie when you go on these trips.

CHARLES. I can never figure out which tie goes with what.

ANNE. This one will look just fine.

CHARLES. If you say so, okay.

(She turns back to us.)

ANNE. *(out)* It was all a wonderful time for Charles — the work, the atmosphere, the enthusiasm; thrilling! *(then)* Until they reached the German countryside. Where they toured a rocket factory. Where there had been a work camp during the war years.

PRISONER. There were roughly fifteen thousand of us here at any given time.

(A young former PRISONER appears. He wears tan work clothes.)

ANNE. Where men and women had been imprisoned.

(The PRISONER moves to CHARLES. ANNE goes.)

PRISONER. The work was mostly assembly-line tasks. Nothing brutal, like at the other camps.

CHARLES. Where are you from originally?

PRISONER. Poland, sir. They're paying me to stay on and help tear the buildings down.

CHARLES. And how long were you, um, held here?

PRISONER. I've been here two years. *(pointing)* Over there's where we slept. The structures are gone now, but you can make out where they were.

CHARLES. Rows and rows of bunks, I'd imagine.

PRISONER. We slept on the floor, sir, and we were grateful for that. *(indicating off)* They'd process the new ones way over there. And the factory was beyond that hill — you can see the roof; it's still standing. And that's the crematorium.

(Silence)

CHARLES. And down there...?

PRISONER. Those are the remains.

CHARLES. Of...

PRISONER. Of the ones they killed. They exterminated close to twenty-five thousand Jews here in the past year-and-a-half.

CHARLES. And they're all... down there? In that pit?

PRISONER. Seems hard to believe, doesn't it? It's not very big. They incinerated the bodies, see, after the gas chambers. Very efficient. The Germans appreciate that. Practicality and all. Those people, my people are all ashes and bits of bone now.

CHARLES. My God… Still. You survived.

PRISONER. I worked hard. I was spared.

CHARLES. I, um... I've seen enough. I believe I need to...

(Clumsily, he grabs the PRISONER's arm for support as he weaves.)

CHARLES. You'll forgive me, it's simply that… I suppose I realized these things were going on — *later on*, I mean. Yet it's, well, it's one thing to have intellectual knowledge and quite another to stand on the scene yourself… *(then)* I've known many Germans, you understand. Many fine, good-hearted men.

PRISONER. We can go now, sir.

CHARLES. And I simply cannot believe that they knew of these monstrosities — of the specifics. It's all too inhuman.

PRISONER. The car's this way.

CHARLES. You mustn't misinterpret me! I'm saying I was *deceived*. If the men with whom I was acquainted knew of these ash pits, then they hid the truth from me. I'm sure of it! The men I knew were not aware of these places, these...

PRISONER. Concentration camps.

CHARLES. These prisoner-of-war camps.

PRISONER. They were called "concentration camps," sir.

CHARLES. No, it's important to be specific. Technically speaking, these were holding pens for the prisoners of war who were captured.

PRISONER. Whenever you're ready to leave...

CHARLES. They housed prisoners of war here. Yes?

(The PRISONER doesn't respond. There is a very long beat.)

CHARLES. I'm ready to go.

(As the lights fade to black, we hear a sound design that includes snippets of lines spoken at the end of the first scene of the play: "Cameras... I don't think so"... "Smile for us, Mr. Lindbergh"... "Just one photo, Mr. Lindbergh"... "Say cheese"... "I'M READY TO GO!"

There's a FLASH! And with that, the lights come up fast and full, and we're back at NASA, where we began.

ADAM and the TV REPORTER are there, next to CHARLES, who's momentarily blinded by the flash.)

ADAM. It was just a photograph.

TV REPORTER. I hope you didn't mind.

ADAM. Are you okay?

TV REPORTER. I didn't mean to upset you...

ADAM. I shouldn't have taken your photo. God, they don't allow that. I could get into big trouble.

CHARLES. It's fine. *I'm* fine.

(A little beat)

ADAM. Anyway. The astronauts are waiting. We should go inside.

TV REPORTER. Mr. Lindbergh, if I could just...?

CHARLES. Yes...?

TV REPORTER. There's one other thing I wanted to mention. I've called my producers in New York. And they'd like... well, *we'd* like to do an interview with you while you're here. If you wouldn't mind.

CHARLES. *(smiles a little at that)* Oh, really?

TV REPORTER. A featurette.

CHARLES. *(his hackles up a bit at that)* Is that so...

TV REPORTER. A "where are they now" sort of piece. They're telling me it could air on the national news. *(then)* Worst case: they'd burn it off on a Sunday morning.

CHARLES. I don't want to do that.

TV REPORTER. It's just an interview, sir...

CHARLES. I don't want to be misunderstood here: *My answer is no.*

(A little beat)

TV REPORTER. Well. I'm sorry this didn't work out, Mr. Lindbergh. But it *was*... incredible to meet you. I mean that.

(He goes. A beat)

CHARLES. *(to ADAM)* Would you mind if we rested a bit before going in?

ADAM. Oh. Not at all.

CHARLES. I need to catch my breath. The heat...

ADAM. Sure. Take your time.

CHARLES. Stay with me.

(A beat. Then, CHARLES brightens up a bit at something he spies off.)

CHARLES. Well. Look at that.
ADAM. What?
CHARLES. That little guy darting around there. Very feisty.
ADAM. Sure.
CHARLES. What do you call that?
ADAM. It's a bird.
CHARLES. No, what's it's *name*? It's not a gull really; it's more like a...
ADAM. Sandpiper. It's called a sandpiper.
CHARLES. Right. *(clucking his tongue)* Hello. Hello, there. He's going about his work with quiet dignity.
ADAM. *(with a smirk)* With all due respect, sir, sandpipers are like the pigeons of southern Florida.
CHARLES. I see...
ADAM. It's not like they're eagles. It's not like they're rare.
CHARLES. I wish we had something to feed him.

(A beat)

ADAM. You ready to go?
CHARLES. You go on in. I'll be right behind you.
ADAM. *(little smile)* I'm supposed to escort you, sir.
CHARLES. I can find my own way.

(ADAM goes. CHARLES stands alone for a moment.)

CHARLES. *(off, to the bird)* Well, hello. There's really something quite regal about you, my good fellow. Something very proud. So they tell me a sandpiper is a sandpiper is a sandpiper. Well, between you and me? A sandpiper is a sandpiper is an eagle. Is an angel. Is to be spared from all this. Which is precisely why you must fly away, my friend. Because you *can*.

Fly away, little sandpiper. Go on. Please.

Yes, fly.

Fly.

Fly...

(The lights fade to black.)

THE END

PROP PLOT

ACT ONE

NASA scene
Rolling metal cart
Small transistor radio (sound comes through it)
Clipboard with papers
Nurse's penlight
Stethoscope
Tongue depressor (perishable)
Large paper bag (filled with freeze-dried food packs that we don't see)
Flash camera circa 1968 (working flash)

Reporter's monologue / Paris scene
Reporter's notepad
Pencil
Sharpener
Louis XVI twin bed
Pocket watch (for Valet)
Bedclothes (sheets, blanket, pillows, pillowcases, etc.)
Elegant coffee cup and saucer
Small tray
Copy of *The New York Times* circa 1927

Cuernavaca scene
Stone bench
2 champagne flutes
Champagne (to fill glasses)

Kidnapping "radio play"
3 1930's-era microphones on stands

Kidnapping press conference scene
Period camera circa 1930's (working flash)
Reporter's notepad
Pencil

Final Charles/Anne scene
Baby's sun suit with American flag on chest

ACT TWO

Reporter's radio address
1030's-era microphone on stand (same as one from Act One)

Next Day Hill scene
Manuscript pages

Rockefeller Institute scene
Rolling cart from NASA scene, redressed with test tubes and other scientific paraphernalia

Barn scene
Wooden cart dressed with the following:
  Massive book
  Test tubes
  Small cage of mice (not seen)

American Ambassador to Germany scene
2 cocktail glasses (filled)
Small red box
Service cross on ribbon (placed in red box)

Aquitania scene
Suitcase
Books
Passport

Reporter's 1939 radio address
Period microphone on stand with NBC banner (redressed from Act One microphone)

Martha's Vineyard scene
Typewritten pages

Charles/Anne post-war scene
Men's jacket

THE GENERAL FROM AMERICA

Richard Nelson

The Tony award-winning playwright of *James Joyce's The Dead* draws a captivating, iconoclastic portrait of America's quintessential traitor, Benedict Arnold. The focus is on how and why a military hero who nearly gave his life for the cause of American freedom disclosed vital information to the British. First produced by the Royal Shakespeare Company and in Houston and New York by The Alley Theatre, this is a rewarding look at intrigue in American history. "Takes a Shakespearean approach to Arnold's character.... It exposes the puritanical hypocrisy and corruption that marched beside the heralded courage of our national beginnings."—*Village Voice.* 11 m., 3 f. (#8995)

JUDGMENT AT NUREMBERG

Abby Mann

Maximilian Schell and George Grizzard starred on Broadway in this powerful stage version of the Academy Award-winning film. Issues at the forefront of this trial reverberate through history and challenge humanity to this day. "A powerful work of art."—*AP*. "Gives oratory the muscle, sweat and high stakes of a last man standing prize fight."—*The New York Times*. "Retains its power to move and provoke us."—*Time*. "A powerhouse."—*Newsday*. "Gripping edge-of-the-seat drama."—Walter Cronkite. "Incisive, blistering, thought-provoking.... Crises out powerfully to our own time in countless ways."—*Chicago Sun-Times*. 15 m., 4 f. (#12919)

GOOD BOYS

Jane Martin

A fierce encounter between fathers, one black and one white, opens a deeply disturbing chapter in their lives. The men relive the school shooting in which their sons died, one a victim and the other the shooter. When racial issues threaten to derail all hope for understanding and forgiveness, the black father's other son pushes the confrontation to a dangerous and frightening climax. This topical drama by the author of *Keely and Du* and other contemporary hits premiered at the Guthrie Theater. "Galvanizing."—*St. Paul Pioneer*. "A terrifying, terrific piece of theatre that is as memorable as it is unsettling."—*Star Tribune*. (#9935)

THE ANASTASIA TRIALS IN THE COURT OF WOMEN

Carolyn Gage

This farcical play-within-a-play is an excursion into a world of survivors and abusers. It opens as a feminist theatre group is about to put sisterhood to an iron test: each draws the role she will play on this evening from a hat. The performance that follows is the conspiracy trial of five women accused of denying Anastasia Romanov her identity. The audience votes to overrule or sustain each motion, creating a different play at every performance. "Farce, social history, debate play, agitprop, audience-participation melodrama, satire [that] makes the head reel!"—*San Diego Union-Tribune*. Wild."—*Washington Blade*. 9 f. (#3742)